Praise
Freedom from Busy

"Flip to any chapter of this book and start feeling good now!"
–Genevieve Parker Hill, Author, *Experience Over Stuff*

"Permission to exhale from the first page. Freedom From Busy is a soul-nourishing guide to chasing your purpose with more ease."
–Sheila Botelho, Health Coach, and host of *The Connect With Sheila Botelho Podcast*

"Like a conversation with a good friend you can expect plenty of relatable YESES right from the start."
–Emmeline Boyce, Re:Mind Studio

"Love this book! The combination of stories, humor and actionable ideas make this book a delight! Each chapter contains bite-sized ways to build a better relationship with yourself! A must read."
–Nancy Jane Smith, Author, *The Happier Approach*

"I'm aware that 'busy' is a deep routed default behavior that makes me feel purposeful, and deep routed in our culture, but I hadn't found many tools

that I can put into practice that actually make profound changes in my behavior just yet. This book is filled with resources that enable you to easily take action and do just what it says on the cover—free yourself from busy. If you're someone who has a default setting of 'busy' then this is a must-read!"
–Liz Spears, Wellness Marketing Consultant and Coach

"Stylish, beautifully written and down to earth. It's like having a GPS to connect to your joy for life no matter what and this is priceless."
–Gaëlle Berruel, Founder of A Rockstar Mindset and host of the Rockstar Mindset Podcast

"Easy and simple, yet profound, exercises that help to change your mindset and increase your joy."
–Patricia Panasri, Astrologer and Business Mentor

"A really enjoyable and delightful read with lots of juicy tips for creating a less busy way of being."
–Rachael Morley, Founder of The Herbalist Hub and Virtually Mindful

"Danielle takes you by the hand and shows you how to release control and sprinkle joy on your daily life. It's like having a personal coaching session throughout the book. Danielle's approach to joy is easy, practical and inspiring."
–Hilda Lorena Tuñon, Integrative Health Coach

FREEDOM
FROM BUSY

FREEDOM *FROM* BUSY

Practical Strategies to Release Your Inner Control Freak and Reclaim Your Joy

Danielle Brooker

The Daisy Patch Publishing.

Freedom From Busy by Danielle Brooker.

Published by The Daisy Patch Publishing, London, United Kingdom. www.thedaisypatch.co.uk.

Copyright © 2021 Danielle Brooker.

Cover design: Genevieve Parker Hill and Jade Roughton.
Interior design: Danielle Brooker.

All rights reserved. No portion of this book may be reproduced by any mechanical, photographics or electronic process, or in the form of a phonographic recording; nor may it be copied for public or private use, other than for 'fair use' as brief quotations embodied in articles and reviews, without prior permission of the publisher.

For permission requests, please write to:
danielle@thedaisypatch.co.uk.

ISBN: 9798590927067

*To Nate, for your effervescent joy.
I love doing life with you. x*

Contents

Introduction 1

Chapter 1: Finding Your Superpowers 5

Chapter 2: The Three Versions of You 15

Chapter 3: Loving Your Growth Nerves 27

Chapter 4: Freedom from Busy 34

Chapter 5: Making It Easy 41

Chapter 6: What Affirmations Are Really About 50

Chapter 7: Getting Out of Your Head and Into Your Heart 58

Chapter 8: Why Your Emotions Matter and How to Get Okay with Them 67

Chapter 9: How to Not Get Swept Up in Others' Emotions 77

Chapter 10: Figuring Out What Lights You Up 86

Chapter 11: The Simple Shift That'll Give You Back Control 94

Chapter 12: The Thing That's Stopping Your Joy 104

Chapter 13:	How to Build Confidence in Yourself	112
Chapter 14:	Getting Cyclical About Life	119
Chapter 15:	How to Choose Joy When You'd Rather Have a Tantrum	131

BONUS CHAPTER:
Overthinking and Getting Unstuck 140

Acknowledgements 147

About the Author 149

Introduction

Welcome, beautiful reader.

I'm Danielle Brooker, life coach and founder of The Daisy Patch, where I guide busy, always-on women to ditch their stress and reclaim their joy.

I believe that so many of us are holding tight to busy as a way to feel more in control of our lives. If we're busy, we don't have to feel the stress, exhaustion, or disconnection that's nagging at us. But, if we're holding back on facing our discomfort, we're also holding back on our deep sense of joy.

It's my calling to remind you that your deep sense of joy can lead you back to yourself. *It's our joy, our fun, and our pleasure in life where we truly come alive.* So that's what this book is all about. And I'm so happy you're here, with it in your hands.

I'll be sharing inspiring stories, tips, strategies, and practical advice to help you create a life that completely lights you up, so you can quit busy for good and still achieve all that you want. Every tool or strategy I share has been incredibly beneficial in my life or for my clients.

Naturally, I'm someone who's constantly engaged in learning and personal growth, and I always want to be able to apply what I'm learning immediately in my life. What I've found throughout my journey is the more that I can learn from others who have been there, done that, or had some sort of experience that I can resonate with, is that my own insights and results get accelerated. Engaging with someone else's *story*, for example, not just a mentor's *advice*, but the story of how they've applied it in their life can really turbocharge our growth. That, in turn, makes our experience of life so much more fun and joyful. Therefore, with this book, I'll be sharing insights and strategies, along with stories of how these concepts have been applied in my life or in my clients' lives.

I know that if you're reading this right now, chances are, you probably resonate or identify with being a high achiever. You want to do well. You want to accomplish things. And you probably also love learning, reading, and growing, right?

What's really cool about loving personal growth is that we're constantly acquiring knowledge. But knowledge without action loses its *oomph*. Knowledge *with* action is where you really get power; it's where the change actually starts to happen.

So, what I'd love to encourage is that you take action when a certain point within these pages resonates with you. Ask yourself, "What could I take away from this?" or, "What's the one thing in this chapter that really sparks something in me?" Then take action.

Taking action can take significant effort. Or it can be as simple as changing your state of mind. It can mean looking at things slightly differently or having a new perspective.

I've structured this book in a way that will be valuable for you no matter what stage you are at—whether you are feeling stuck and lost, exhausted with competing pressures in your life, inspired and ready to take action, or going through any time of transition and change. See this as a handy, quick guidebook to bring you back to center. As my friend Liz said, it's like a "pep talk in your pocket."

Throughout each chapter, I'll walk you through simple, practical, and heart-led tools that'll not only give you relief from busy but support you to completely transform your relationship with busyness for good. You could pick the book up and turn to the chapter that resonates most for you at the time or read it the whole way through—it's entirely up to you.

I'm not one for short-term fixes and playing at the surface level. I'm much more interested in creating the kind of change that will get to the root cause of some of your frustrations right now—unlocking you fully. Which is why I promise you this book is full of heart *and* strategy. A potent mix for reclaiming your joy, so you can live a life that completely lights you up.

Finally, I love hearing from readers. As you make your way through this book, let me know where you are in your journey of freeing yourself from busy. Email me at Danielle@TheDaisyPatch.co.uk.

I've also included additional book resources to fuel your action-taking, which you can download for free at www.FreedomFromBusy.com/gifts.

Now, let's dive in!

Chapter 1:

Finding Your Superpowers

Twelve years ago, I was completely lost. From the outside looking in, I was doing great. But on the inside, I was *stuck*. I desperately wanted clarity on my next step, yet had no idea how to move forward.

I know that I'm not alone in this feeling. I'd love to count the number of times I've heard anyone—friends, family, clients, come to me and say, "I feel stuck. I'm lost and have no idea what my next step is. What should I do?"

There have been times in my life where the feeling of being stuck has been big, and times in my life where it's been just a little bump in my day. But I think we've all gone through moments where our head is a little bit clouded. We feel disconnected.

There's a lot of power in clarity.

What I tend to find in those moments when I'm feeling stuck is that what I'm really feeling is completely separated from knowing *the thing that's going to spark joy for me again*. There's no clarity. I've lost touch with the stuff that I know – and only I can know, it's very unique to me – will light me up again, spark the fire in my heart, and get me excited and smiling or skipping along the street again.

In the disconnected times, I feel like I've lost touch with who I am. I know that's quite a big, grandiose statement to make, but what I mean is that it feels like something's disconnected, and I want to plug back in.

Do you feel like *you've lost that spark*? Like if you could *plug yourself back in again*, you could get going again? Decisions would be easier. Things would flow. That "stuckness" feeling wouldn't be there anymore.

If I told you that you could tap into that energy source that you're craving and light yourself up again, what would you do? I'm sure you're saying to yourself, *yes, please, I want that!*

The concept of knowing your superpowers had been familiar to me, but it wasn't until I heard it described by one of my beautiful mentors that I really got its significance. Look her up; her name is Marie Forleo. She's a coach extraordinaire and a whole bunch of other things. I'm not going to do her justice in this short chapter. Go Google her, please. She's got exceptional content over on her MarieTV YouTube channel, with a lot of tools that I've used and that you can use as well.

I've done variations of this exercise in some way, shape, or form at particular turning points in my life. I have always naturally gravitated toward wanting to know my unique strengths. What the exercise I'm about to describe helps me draw to the surface is *clarity*. It gives me concrete examples of my superpowers that I can then refer back to.

The exercise is really quite simple. It's as simple as asking yourself, "What are my superpowers?" That's it. Profound and simple. It's asking yourself and others, as you'll see in a minute, *what are my superpowers?*

Your superpowers are those unique qualities about you, those unique strengths that make you, you. When you walk in the room, what changes? What makes you who you are? What are the things that your friends say they love about you?

You can ask yourself this question, and you might have a couple of answers, or you might feel really weird. You might not know how to draw the answers out of yourself. It's more than the interview question, "What are your strengths?" We're looking for your superpowers. They're not your strengths or skills, exactly. Your superpowers are the innate qualities and characteristics that make you who you are.

The really cool, fun part of the exercise that I got so much value out of is to actually reach out to friends, family, and colleagues. Reach out to people who have been part of your life in many different spheres. Include close friends as well as acquaintances. Pose the question to them like you're doing a mini survey.

We can be so stuck in our heads and in self-doubt mode that it's not often we allow ourselves to receive external feedback in a really loving, compassionate way. Posing the superpowers question to people in your life in a very specific way helps them to reflect love and compassion back to you.

I'm inviting you to reach out to 10, 20, or 30 people. Make it a number big enough that it makes you feel uncomfortable. It's a data-mining exercise. Ask these people, "What do you think my three superpowers are?"

That's it. You can tell them, "I don't need you to write me a huge email, just the first three things that pop into your head. I don't need you to think that hard about it. The first response is the right response."

What I found when I started to receive these responses back was not only did I feel really good – I'm not going to lie, it's a very fun activity to get some feel-goods – but that innately, deep in my body, I agreed with them. I could see what they were saying. *Oh yeah, that is true about me.*

One of the ones that kept coming up in slightly different wording, was essentially about my thoughtfulness. I remember birthdays. I remember things that people have told me, and I check in with them. And that is one of the things that make me who I am. I enjoy being thoughtful. Not only does it bring me joy and light me up, but it is also part of who I am.

What happens after you see all of the responses is that there are general things you will notice that you can start to group together in different categories. Compare the two lists, the one you did on your own and the one you got through the mini survey. Chances are, you're going to come out with a list of two, three, four, or five superpowers. These are your innate qualities, the things that make you who you are, the things that turbo-charge you in the world.

Now, why are we talking about superpowers? How do use your superpowers? Why even bother going to this level of detail in your life?

Too often, when we reach a frustrating stuck point, there's this immediate response that kicks in that is your brain in fix-it mode. Your brain says, *let's resolve this, there's a little blip, let's clear it and move forward.* We try to fix it with busyness. You move on, but it's not really addressed. You get a little bit of relief in the moment, but you circle back to the same issue again.

Have you ever noticed how you might have a really stuck day about an issue at work? Then a few weeks later, you realize you're having that same conversation again, and it's still bothering you? This is because we haven't got to the deeper level, the real root cause of things.

The stuckness, the frustration, the clouded feeling that comes over us can sound like these thoughts:

- How do I make this next decision?
- How do I move forward with my life?
- How do I amplify?
- How do I not just grow but make the most of things?
- I'm feeling like things are okay, but they could be better.

I believe these thoughts come with a stuck feeling when we've disconnected from our light. We've disconnected from what makes us who we are. We've disconnected from our superpowers.

If you're trying to reconnect to something, if you're trying to plug something back in, you're going to have to know what the plug is, or where the plug is, or how to recognize the plug in the first place.

So, to charge yourself back up, connect back in with yourself. I know that it can be frustrating to have someone say to you, "You have to get to know who you are." But, a lot of the time, when we're in a stuck state of mind, our brain is concentrated on *get-unstuck-get-unstuck-get-unstuck*. It's not as if a post-it note pops up in our heads and reminds us who we are. We have to dig beneath the surface, and for many of us, it's not something we've had to do for many years, maybe in our entire lifetime.

I believe that the light, the energy, the joy, the spice of life is when we are being who we are. When we are plugged back in.

So, why bother with superpowers? Well, if you're stuck, and if you know you're at A, and you know you need to get to B, but you don't know the steps, that first step could be to get to know who you are. Get a little bit more information about B so that you can move toward it. I really believe that the superpowers exercise I've shared here does that. It helps you to get to know yourself on a deeper level.

When I first did this exercise in this particular way, it was about three years ago. Now, I've done a lot of personal growth. I've done a lot of self-help reading and integration in my own life. I've always been that person sitting in the front of the class, wanting to sign up to the extra training course. And, I've had *some* levels of clarity on what my strengths are over the years. I've been clear on the things that make me who I am, and I feel like I had a great list of things that light me up in my life.

Yet, it wasn't until I did **this specific exercise in the specific way I describe here** that I had much more clarity in my life and how I could start to show up in my business or in my personal life in a specific way.

Let me give you an example. I've been through varying emotional relationships with my thoughtfulness. For example, I've mentioned before that I love remembering people's birthdays. And I do. It really lights me up to make someone feel special. I like to send a little message or a card or call someone on their birthday to make them feel loved. It's a little thing that's personal to me. It makes me who I am.

I've gone on and off again with my relationship with my thoughtfulness and how I express it. At times, I've been frustrated with the effort it takes to remember birthdays. My inner monologue would sound like: *Why am I doing this? This is too stressful.* I've taken a break and not done it at all, and I've wondered why at the end of that quarter, or six months, or a year, I felt a bit off, a bit "meh." When I paused to think, I realized that one of the things I hadn't done over that period was to send birthday cards.

Now, I know that might sound like a very small, possibly insignificant example to share, but it's relevant. Because the new level of distinction for me around my thoughtfulness being a superpower helped me integrate it more into my life. It helped me appreciate it. My thoughtfulness makes me who I am, and I love that part of me.

Therefore, whatever I'm doing, whether it's in my business, with my coaching clients, creating new content, or engaging in a meaningful conversation with a friend, then my thoughtfulness, if I tap into it, is going to spark me up. It's my connection to the plug point. If I'm feeling a little out of sorts, and I don't have any clarity, and I'm finding it hard to make decisions, maybe I need to tap back into one of my superpowers.

Knowing my superpowers also meant I had more certainty to keep prioritizing them—and feel stronger in saying no to the busyness that would otherwise get in the way.

This is where the articulation of our superpowers—having them written down and memorized—becomes really important. Because the point of this tool, and all the practices I will share in this book, is not only to think about it but to actually take action. Before I heard Marie explain it in her unique way, I hadn't followed through on taking action in getting to know mine.

When you take action, it integrates the knowledge into your life, and that's where the change takes shape. I invite you to try this exercise today, even if you only write yourself a little note right now about your superpowers. What are the first three things that come to mind?

The next time you feel stuck, maybe you won't hang out there for so long because you know your superpowers. The next time you're challenged by a decision you have to make, maybe you'll be gentler and softer with yourself. Maybe the indecision won't last so long. Maybe you'll make a decision that feels incredible for you, and you now know why. You can replicate that feeling over and over and over again.

What could *your* superpowers be? Find out and move forward with clarity.

I would love to know what you've discovered from applying this concept in your life. Send me an email at Danielle@TheDaisyPatch.co.uk with your insights or questions from this chapter or any of the following chapters in this book.

Chapter 2:

The Three Versions of You

Hundreds of years ago, there was this huge Buddha statue in a temple in Thailand. It wasn't of any major significance, other than that it was really big. It was made of stucco plaster. There was nothing particularly special about it, except its large size.

One day, someone was relocating the statue, and it was damaged. A little chip of it fell off. You can imagine they thought, "Oh no, this is terrible. How am I going to patch this precious statue back together?" As they picked up this piece that had fallen off and went to restore it somehow, they noticed something shining through. They noticed where the piece of plaster had fallen away, that what was under it looked a little bit shiny. And they got curious. So they chipped away a little bit more of the plaster. And underneath was a layer of gold.

As it turned out, this huge statue was entirely made of gold. It had been covered up for so long that there was no one around who remembered that it was supposed to be gold, not plaster. There had been an invasion, and the statue was covered over to protect it from being stolen. It worked well—too well. It wasn't until the middle of the 20th century that this outer layer chipped off, and the world discovered there was gold on the inside. If you google "Golden Buddha Statue Thailand," this is what comes up.

I love this story. It relates to how we're feeling when we're particularly stuck and covered up and on autopilot in our lives. We can be like this statue.

I was like the statue for years in my own life. I felt like things were okay. I was sitting there. I had a nice enough life. People may have admired it, but there was not much that felt like *me* there. It was almost as though I was just going through the motions. I had all the boxes ticked: lovely job, lovely home, lovely friends, lovely partner. Life looked really good from the outside. From the inside, there was a different story going on.

On the inside I was feeling fragmented, stuck, and confused. I was asking myself, *is this it? Isn't there more*?

When clients first come to see me, they often say things like, "I'm feeling stuck. I'm feeling a little bit lost. I want to know what my next steps are. I'm feeling like I've lost my spark. I want to get back to myself again."

Many of us have this inkling that we've lost some part of ourselves that we need to get back to. We know deep down inside of us that there's *more*. More light, more energy, more excitement, more *something* to express. That something is the golden core on the inside.

It's like somehow, over the years, we've been covered up with plaster. Maybe it was a protection mechanism that started back when we were little. Maybe you got in trouble for doing something and suddenly thought, *I'd better cover up this gold.*

For me, it's little things, like maybe I sang too loudly in the school classroom, and someone said, "No! Be quiet!" and then I thought, *okay, singing is not what I'm supposed to do.*

This is one of the ways we use busy—to cover ourselves up. Now, so you know, this covering up process is perfectly natural and normal. Whoever covered up the Buddha statue hundreds of years ago was doing the best they could at the time. They thought *this is the best possible approach now. Let's put some protection over this beautiful gold to make sure we keep it safe.*

As we moved from childhood through to adulthood, we went through this process. We were exposed to different threats, and we decided, bit by bit, to cover that beautiful inner gold core.

In the personal development world, you hear a lot about "getting back to your authentic self." When I first heard that phrase, it felt like this lovely, lofty idea. *That sounds nice. I wonder who this authentic self is? I want some of that.* But it also felt distant. I didn't know in practical terms what *authentic self* meant for me or what being it looked like in my life.

However, when this metaphor of the golden Buddha was shared with me, it finally made sense. I'd always felt like there was gold on the inside, I just didn't know how to access it. There were fragments of my days, or months, or years, where I could see that shining light inside of me. That beautiful gold came out to play sometimes. And then it got covered up again.

In this chapter, I want to talk about how those covering layers serve us for a time and how we can now show our gold.

We actually have three selves. We have three different versions of our selves. This is something that many psychology and human behavior texts reference in different ways.

My favorite way is what I'm going to share with you in this chapter. I first learned it in my coaching training with The Coaching Institute, and then again from one of my mentors, the beautiful Sharon Pearson. She's the founder of The Coaching Institute in Australia, which is Australia's number one coaching school, and she's phenomenal.

Firstly, there's the outer layer we show the world. This is the covered-up version. Let's call it *the pretend self*. This is the self that we take out into the big scary world. This is the self that I like to describe as the one I put on as I'm getting ready for the day. I grab my coat and walk out the door. That coat is symbolic of me putting on my layer. This is how I'm going to show up. This is who I am now, this is "professional Danielle." I'm putting on how I want people to perceive me.

This is the image that we project to the world. For me, it was that I'm going to act and behave confidently. I'm going to tune into what my colleagues are saying and act smart. I can think of times in my economics and policy career where I behaved in a way that would portray me being more confident or knowing more about things than I really did. So, if people were talking about a particular thing that was going on in current events, I would give all the facial expressions that would say *yes, oh, that's very interesting*. I would throw in a few buzzwords, perhaps. I wanted to be part of the conversation. I wanted to act smart. This is not to say that I'm not smart or intelligent, but to give the flavor of how that behavior showed up in the moment. Perhaps I wouldn't be clear about the truth, that either A) I wasn't that interested in the conversation, or maybe, B) I didn't know that much about it after all.

There are lots of different ways we put on the pretend self. This could be where you say *yes* to go see a movie that you don't really want to see because your pretend self is afraid that friends might judge you for not liking that genre of movies. Maybe you don't like arthouse films, but they invited you to an arthouse film, and you want to seem likable. It's natural that we do this.

Sometimes we *have* to put this layer on. For example, in work situations, we may have to talk about things we don't necessarily want to talk about. It's part of life. What I'm encouraging through this chapter is simply to identify that these layers *exist*. That these versions of us exist. It's up to us to tune more and more into the inner core—that depth of gold that we know is there.

The second self, the second layer, is *who we're afraid we are*. We can think of this as our *negative self-image*. If something really upsets us, it's usually because, at some level, we believe that it might be true.

For example, my partner might make a joke about me. On some days, perhaps on a tired, grumpy day, I might take offense to that joke. When I ask him about it, he'll say, "I'm just joking." He might have said something like, "Oh, that's so silly," and I heard it as him thinking *I'm* silly and stupid. But what's really happening, if his words are upsetting me, is that at some level, I believe it *could* be true. I believe, *oh, maybe it is true that I'm stupid or silly.*

The negative traits that we're identifying with in those moments are not really ours. It's not that I am stupid or silly. That's a negative self-image. It's the chatter of self-doubt. Often it's stuff that was programmed in when we were little.

Through identifying some of the things that you might be afraid you are, you become able to let them go.

The negative self-image is the underbelly of the top layer, the one we show to the world, the pretend self. For example, I was showing up with my confident attitude of *I know. I've got this. Yes, I know about all these topics.*

Underneath that, there was this layer of, *I'm so afraid they're going to find me out and really see that I'm stupid and don't know what's going on.*

But underneath this negative self-image layer, you get to the core.

Underneath the self-doubt chatter is your authentic self.

Here's what I call my "Friday night example." There have been plenty of times in my life where I've said, "Yes, I want to go out with my friends tonight" on a Friday. But actually, I didn't want to go. What I really wanted to do was go home and relax. I wanted to be on the couch; I wanted to be warm and cozy inside my own house. But I've said "yes" because someone else invited me and I felt this sense of, *I better make sure they're ok. I better make sure I please them. I better make sure they have company.*

The people-pleaser role is one way I could describe my pretend self. For you, perhaps you identify as being the "good-girl." You always want to do the right thing. Or you want to be the hero. You want to be seen to come in and fix things and make things happen (you can see where "busy" starts to show up for us). Each of these versions of ourselves and the behaviors that show up around them are not us operating from the gold. They're versions of us that are cloaks. They're the different, pretend selves that we take out into the world. We use them to hide our negative self-images, but they also hide the gold.

I love the way that Sharon describes our three selves. She refers to these selves in her book, *Ultimate You*, as *the core, the crud,* and *the crust.*

According to Sharon, we've got this crusty outside layer that could easily flake away and get to that more tender part of us, which is the cruddy stuff. The cruddy, mucky, negative self-image that we're afraid that we are, but that is not really who we are. Then we get to the core. That's your gold; that's who you really are.

Now, I've got a few questions for you. So, go get your journal, or mull these over in your mind. I'll share a question for each of the three versions of you.

Each question helps you bring more awareness into your conscious mind. A lot of these behaviors happening in our day-to-day lives are ingrained and on autopilot. We don't even realize we're doing them. It's not like I realized that I was putting on that pretend, confident self I was when I walked out the door each day. The more that you identify why you're doing certain things, the more that you can start to question whether you want to change them or not. And the more that you can bring your core, authentic you out into the world.

Question One

This is to describe your crusty layer (as Sharon puts it), your pretend self, the one that you put out into the world. A really simple way to question yourself here is to simply ask, *how do I like to be seen?*

For me, I liked to be seen as a confident, bubbly, social person. It's not to say that I'm not that person, it's just to say that these became dominant behaviors for me. That's how I wanted to be seen. And often, being seen this way came at the *expense of my own needs*. I would take on too much and get too busy. I'd get stressed out. I'd overcommit. Because I liked to be seen as confident, sociable, and bubbly, it meant that on my down days and on my grumpy days, nobody else could tell how I really felt because I wouldn't put it out in the world.

Question Two

This question is, *what's the opposite of each of those traits of your pretend self?*

I wanted to be seen as confident and bubbly, and always on. So the opposite of that was fearing I'd be seen as lazy or not confident, or not capable. The opposite of what you are putting out into the world is a clue as to what you're afraid of. This is your cruddy layer. It's not what's true about you, but what you are afraid is true about you.

Question Three

This is my favorite question, and I'm sure you've heard variations of this before.

This question identifies who you really are in that beautiful golden core.

Who are you when nobody is watching?

For me, my golden core is what I call my *sofa self*. When nobody is watching, I am grounded, calm, and quiet. I'm really quiet when nobody's watching until, of course, the music gets going, and then I can be silly and fun!

When I first asked myself this question, my quiet calmness came up and surprised me because I would usually show up in a very social, big, bubbly way. Again, not to say that I'm not also social and bubbly, but what I want you to hear is that when nobody is watching, I'm actually quite happy to be on the couch, reading and delighting in it. I'm watching *Friends* episodes on repeat and laughing my head off. I'm reading self-help books and loving it. This was part of me that I would not have put out there.

When you're feeling stuck, it's likely that you have knocked up against one of your false selves. There's a chip that's fallen off your pretend self that's reminding you there's something to be discovered. There's something shining inside that you want to tune into even more. Lean into that. The only way to lean in here is to become more aware of what's going on. To know that these selves exist. To reacquaint yourself with your beautiful, shining core. I trust that some of these questions will be a golden opportunity for you to chip away at the plaster a little bit more.

Bring awareness into your life that there could be a few different versions of you. If you start to get curious about those different versions and how they show up in your world, then that will help you reconnect to the real you and the big, beautiful, light inside.

Chapter 3:

Loving Your Growth Nerves

I love walking. If I miss my daily walk, I'll feel mentally clouded the next day. I love the gentleness of the movement. I love being outside and being by water if I can. Walking along the water always helps me feel calm and refreshed.

The running joke with a few friends is that my kind of yoga is child's pose. That's what makes me feel good. That's the type of movement that works for me. And child's pose is actually stillness and rest.

Then, about a year and a half ago, something began building in my body. I began feeling a need for heightened physical movement—something more than gentle walking and child's pose.

I've always really loved music and I'm a mad musicals fan. I get this feeling after I see a show like, *I want to be up on stage and be singing and dancing with them.* I also grew up with beautiful older sisters who were dancers. So, there's another running joke, this one in my family, that I have two left feet. I don't really mind that I'm not the most coordinated person. I love the way I dance, and it doesn't really matter, but growing up there was this chatter in my head that said, *oh no! I'm not good at this!*

But I still love it. And I had this feeling that I needed to do something different for my exercise. I'm not about to go into a hard-core intensity training session at the gym. I know that's not for me and my body. I'm very mindful of what works for me. I just really wanted to dance.

There's a great dance studio in my area. On and off for a while, I'd look them up and think, *maybe I could go take classes there*. They teach musical jazz and hip hop. I'd often secretly research the studio. *Wouldn't that be fun?* I'd think, but I wasn't ready to tell anyone about my desire to attend classes there yet.

Every time I looked it up, or even walked past, it stirred something in my body. The studio is a place where a lot of the West End performers train. I would imagine what it would feel like to walk in there, and feel the music, and be surrounded by all these elite dancers, and have a window into their life and their theatrical experience. This studio also offers public classes open to everyone, from absolute beginners through to professional dancers.

And one day, about a year and a half ago, I finally booked into one of these classes. I don't know exactly what made me book, but I think it was a combination of my diary being open, listening to some tunes at home, and feeling a little out of alignment physically.

So I did it. I signed up. I walked in and paid my money. As I walked up to the class, I could see that there was a line of people waiting to go into the studio. I started comparing myself to them. I'm thinking, *these people are a lot younger than me, and oh, they've got fancy clothes on, and oh, look at their fancy shoes.* I was in my old yoga pants and runners.

Then it's time. I walk into the class with about thirty other people and the music starts pumping. Up until this point, I was happy to observe. My body was pretty calm. When the music started, I positioned myself at the back of the room.

And then I feel this sensation changing in my body. I'm getting a little bit tingly. I notice that I'm constantly looking around, watching everyone around me. My heart's beating faster. And I notice that I'm shrinking my body; my shoulders are tucked a little bit. But I'm also smiling a tiny bit; there's a little smirk on my face.

Here's what is going on in my head:

My inner dialogue is saying, "Oh, my God, what are you doing? Look, they know what they're doing. Oh, they just stepped to the right. Have we started? I wonder if they're watching. Should I have my shoes on? Should I have my shoes off? What should I do?"

I was smiling to myself because I was *noticing* my inner chatter. And at the end of each of these panicked thoughts, there was this other voice that was saying, with a gentle laugh, "Nobody's watching you."

For a moment, I was caught up with anxiety. My skin was hot, there was tightness in my chest, and my belly was fluttery. I was jittery and nervous. I was starting to worry so much about what other people were thinking of me. And then I was able to laugh because it was so cool that my mind in that moment also went, *and nobody's watching you.*

It was an ego check. *This ain't about you.* Every time I had a self-doubting thought, like, *what are you even doing here?* I also had the voice that said, "Nobody's watching you. You're here for a reason. Keep going. You don't have to get it right. This is about fun."

Once I began to focus on *fun*, I started paying attention to the music, letting it wash over me and get into my bones. Other dancers were going right, and I was going left, and it didn't matter. I was having fun. I began to feel amazed at the energy of that room, the enthusiasm of the other dancers, and the skill of the teacher.

There was a peak in my nervousness at the beginning of the class. It was the most self-conscious I had been for as long as I could remember. Yet, as I walked away from the class, all I could do was smile. I was beaming from ear to ear. I felt energized and excited like a happy toddler. But at first, it was really scary. And that might sound weird to some people, that a dance class would be scary. But to me, it was. I had to confront how much I didn't know. I was an absolute beginner.

The experience was a reminder to me that everything is a journey. That the body sends us cues. That just because we're nervous does not mean we need to stop. Just because we're fearful or full of self-doubt, does not mean we need to stop. Because in addition to the fear, there was excitement. In fact, the nervousness and self-consciousness transformed into feelings of, *oh, my God! I'm doing a dance class! I love dancing. I love music. I'm here. I did it.*

I recognized that there is a journey to learning and growth. I can make the choice to keep showing up in the room. To keep learning more dance moves. And it will get easier; I will feel better.

It was also a reminder of the other times in my life where I have shown up in a room and felt incredibly nervous. Maybe it's on the first day of meeting a brand-new team in a brand-new role at work. Maybe it's being in a job interview where I've had to sit a test beforehand, and I don't know what's going to happen.

I shared this story of my dance class nerves with my beautiful accountability buddy, Julie, fairly soon after the event. We began sharing different scenarios in our lives where a similar feeling has shown up, and we started to laugh and celebrate each other because we have learned to love the feeling. We decided to call this feeling "growth nerves." We recognize when our growth nerves show up and we say, "Hey! This is nervousness, this is fear, this is scared."

I can distinguish between that nervousness that kicks in when I'm growing, stretching, and evolving myself, versus the anxiousness that is a legitimate fear, like if I'm about to cross the road and there's a bus coming. There's a distinct difference.

I invite you to start getting to know the difference between the two types of fear in your own life. When are you feeling growth nerves about something you haven't tried before or something that is fairly new to you? Of course you're not supposed to know all of the steps. It's brand new. How can you learn to notice that feeling and celebrate it?

Busyness takes over as a way to block that 'scary,' self-conscious feeling. If I busy myself, I get to distract myself from what's going on (or avoid it all together). So, if I give it a name, if I call it *growth nerves*, I get to still feel nervous, because that's natural. I certainly wasn't able to shake that feeling in that dance class. But I also get to pin it to growth. I get to know that I can feel this way now, and then when I do it again, it's going to feel different, until the nervousness fades away and I'm fully integrated.

Get to know what your own growth nerves feel like so that when they show up, you don't slam on the breaks and immediately stop what you're doing. Recognizing growth nerves allows you to keep going. Remind yourself that the more *competent* you become at something, the more *confident* you become at something. Maybe it's a dance class. Maybe it's not. Maybe you're laughing at my two left feet in this chapter. That's fine.

Your results come from turning the insight that you're taking away from this chapter into some sort of action and integration in your life. Begin to look for opportunities to feel your growth nerves and label them so that you can move forward and fully connect with what brings you joy and fun in life.

Chapter 4:

Freedom from Busy

You could say my specialty is supporting people who have a lot on their plate.

Maybe you have a lot of projects on and have been working overtime; maybe you feel like you're never really getting ahead. You're ending the day feeling exhausted. And then there's still the non-work stuff to deal with too. You still want to have a social life. You still want to take care of your friends and family and yourself. How do you fit in exercise?

Much of the time, the conversation around busyness tends to gravitate toward our schedules. What have I got on? How could I remove something to reduce some of the pressure? How could I rearrange my diary to feel more spacious and relaxed?

While I'm a big believer in creating a lot of spaciousness in your diary, what happens when you do that and *still* feel busy? What happens when you still feel stressed?

Recently, I was having a conversation with my partner on one of our afternoon walks. I said, "You know, I have all these things going on, and I'm feeling busy." Then I literally stopped myself in my tracks. *Hang on a second. I'm someone who teaches people how to break up with busy. I don't actually use the word "busy" very often. What's going on here?*

I've mostly removed "busy" from my vocabulary because I've designed and created my life and schedule based on how I want to feel on a daily basis. My schedule now supports and optimizes my favorite emotional experiences. So the fact that the word *busy* slipped out of my mouth caught me by surprise. I had to question it. When I started to explain the feeling to my partner, the words that came out of my mouth were, "I'm not actually busy. I've got tons of spaciousness in my diary. I get to choose when I have meetings. I love that side of things. The busyness is actually the state of my *mind* right now."

Have you ever experienced telling yourself any of the following?

- I'm so busy because there's too much on at work.
- I'm so busy because family life is chaotic.
- I'm so busy because I'm trying to up my exercise regime.
- I'm so busy because my company is so disorganized and unsupportive.

What if the busyness is actually a state of your mind and has very little to do with your *things to do* list?

What I want to invite you to consider in this chapter is: what if your freedom from busy pathway wasn't about your workload?

Any time when you'd typically use the words *busy* and *stressed* to describe your situation, I want you to check in and ask yourself: *where is this busyness coming from?*

Try to identify the *location* of the busyness. Are you actually busy? Or is this a state of mind? Is the busyness taking place in your mind? If you were to pause and let me peer into your mind for a moment, what would it look like? Maybe your mind is like a room where people are coming and going and setting up plates and dropping plates, and different types of music are pumping.

When you bring awareness to *where* the busyness is, you can actually start to release some of it. When you're getting to the deep root cause of feeling of busy—whatever and however that shows up for you—you can *choose* to release it.

Now, I know that sounds easier said than done. *How do I just release it?* You tell a busy person to stop being busy or take something off their things to do list, and that can lead them straight into panic mode. (I know—because that used to be me).

However, when you can acknowledge the busyness could be happening in your mind, you can also invite in the question: *how could I release some of this busyness?*

Maybe the busyness is that you're trying to plan a holiday while also planning your meals for the week, grocery shopping online, remembering to call your mom, and trying to solve all of your work problems before Monday morning.

Now, when you can identify that that's a lot going on in your mind, and you ask yourself, *what if I could release it*, what happens?

Maybe you could release some of the meal stuff because you don't need to figure that out right now. Or maybe you could release everything and tell yourself that actually, all of this doesn't need to be resolved today.

When I went through this process with myself recently, the acknowledgment that my *mind* was busy was a release *in itself*. Awareness is enough to click things over and give you a whole new perspective, which immediately brings in a softening of the hard, busy feeling.

If I could distill my teaching down to one vital point, it would be the concept of getting out of your head and into your heart. It's a softening process.

Back at university, I happened to have two of my besties studying the same course with me. We'd have incredible study sessions. We'd all gather around one of our dining room tables. We tended to have a bit of a ritual about it. Someone would bring the chocolate. There would always be tons of tea available. We always lit a tealight candle that heated a wax melt infused with these beautiful-smelling essential oils. The oil-infused wax melts had a flat circular shape. They're quite hard to begin with, though they still smell pretty. You put them on top of this glass bit where the candle's melting them, and slowly and surely, they soften. They release. And then they turn into this liquid that fills the room with a gorgeous scent.

It's this kind of process that I imagine when I think about moving from my head into my heart. The head is nice; it's got a pleasant smell, but it's also got a hardness and a rigidity to it when we stay there. How can I support my emotions to relax and soften by moving into my heart space? By releasing some of the hardness of being stuck in your head, you can experience the liquid melted goodness of the heart.

In her book, *Warrior Goddess Training*, HeatherAsh Amara talks a lot about the work of the HeartMath

Institute. Their various techniques are all based on the science of strengthening the vital connection between the heart and mind. Showing that the heart actually sends far more messages (orders) to the brain than the other way round. HeatherAsh shares what she has learned from HeartMath, writing, "The heart has 40,000 neurons—as many as the brain. And when the heart leads, the mind becomes more focused and relaxed."

Isn't that what we're all craving? A sense of being both focused *and* relaxed? What's happening when we have created busyness in our mind is that we've actually created hardness. We're not relaxed, and therefore, we're not focused either. I'll go even deeper on getting out of your head and into your heart later, in Chapter Seven.

Anytime that you have a conversation about busyness, either with yourself or with others, and anytime you're considering your diary management, ask yourself, "Have I considered the management of the busyness of my mind? How many thoughts am I trying to figure out at the same time?"

I often say to my partner, "Can we close that tab now?" If we're having multiple conversations, there's too much going on. Let's close some of our metaphorical internet browser tabs.

What tabs do you need to close in your mind?

Close those tabs and melt down into your heart to create the feelings you're craving: relief, focus, relaxation, and freedom from busy, once and for all.

Chapter 5:

Making It Easy

So, you're overwhelmed.

You've taken on *way* too much. Maybe you have multiple deadlines at work. The projects at work are piling up. You really want to do a good job, but you've also overcommitted on your social schedule, you haven't exercised in weeks, and you can feel the pressure mounting.

There's stress. There's pressure. Just writing about it now, I can almost feel anxiety in my chest thinking of moments like this in my own life.

What I notice about overwhelm, as it creeps up on us, is that we start to make the problem bigger than it needs to be. When we start to focus on all of the things on our to-do list, on all the deadlines and expectations, it can feel monumental. Creating our dreams or goals can feel unachievable and unattainable. We may have big goals—earn one million dollars, buy that dream house, take a year off, start that business, or travel the world, for example. These goals can feel nice, but they can also feel too in-the-distance, and because of that, we're not attached to them, and we don't take action.

In my coaching sessions, what I often say to my clients is, "If something's too big, we're not going to take actions toward it. We're going to get stuck. We're going to see this huge thing and think, *there's no way I can do this.*" And so, we get stuck in the same spot. And we spin in place. Those feelings of overwhelm grow bigger and bigger. The longer we stay standing still, the more overwhelming everything is because that deadline becomes looming, or the thought of getting started in itself is suddenly magnified.

Now, it's in these particular moments that I say what we need to do if we're going to take action is to *chunk it down*.

Even writing that now makes me feel better.

Chunk it down.

Ask yourself:

- How could I make this simpler?
- How could I take one tiny, weeny little step toward this goal?
- What's the smallest possible thing that I could do?

If you're standing still, the overwhelm and anxiety just gets bigger. If you're standing still, that dream of traveling the world, starting that business, taking a year off, or earning a million dollars is even further away.

Right?

It's never going to happen if you're standing still.

The only time that you feel unstuck, the only time you feel you have direction, clarity, and confidence, is when you're in motion. It's when you're taking action.

I believe that what gets us stuck again is when we try to take too big an action. Creating unnecessary busyness. We fail, and then we beat ourselves up about that.

For example, when I sit down to write my to-do list. On a daily basis, I set myself just three priorities—three things that need to happen in the day. This is part of a planning technique that I use.

Last week, I wrote down my three things, and they were BIG things. They were *monumental* things. And I thought, *yeah, I'm going to do it all!* I felt great at the start of the day. Well, I got to the end of the day, I looked at my list, and I'd barely even touched on the first thing in my list. I had barely made *ten percent* of progress on item number one. I proceeded to think, *I'm a terrible person, I'm terrible at my job, I cannot believe I didn't do any of these things*. I started the self-doubt loop.

Isn't it funny how we do this to ourselves? We set ourselves up for failure, so it's no wonder we get back to feeling so stuck.

What if, instead of beating yourself up over all the things you didn't do, because you set them too monumentally in the first place, you asked yourself:

What if things could be really easy?

And,

What would make *this* easy?

For you to take action toward the thing that you want, whether it's the big, lofty dream or simply wanting to finish a project, ask yourself:

What is one thing I could do? And how could that one thing be really super-duper easy?

John Assaraf runs an organization called NeuroGym. He is a world-leading coach, and what I love about him is that he hangs out with neuroscientists. This means he understands a lot about human behavior, and more specifically, he understands a lot about the human mind and how the brain works. In an interview with Lewis Howes, founder and CEO of The School of Greatness, John was sharing the power of creating habits.

Habits are actions we do over and over again, until they become so ingrained that they're automatic to us. A lot of the time, when we're talking about creating change in our lives or working toward a goal or a dream, we want to create supportive habits. For example, if you want to get fit and healthy, then you need to change your habits. Maybe you need to wake up early and go for a daily walk or take some time to plan out healthy meals each week.

What John shared in his interview with Lewis blew my mind. I'd heard this concept explained in different ways before, but the way he shared about it in this particular interview helped cement it for me.

John described how the brain is essentially a muscle and that if you want to create habits, the most powerful way to do it, and the only successful way, is to start as small as possible.

He shared an example. If you want to be able to do 100 pushups, the best possible way to make sure that you succeed at that, is *not* to get up on day one and do 50 pushups and then get up on day two, and realize you are sore and you can only make it to 20, and then get up on day three and do two pushups, and then get up on day four and tell yourself you're a really terrible person and you're never going to try that again and you'll never follow through and never be fit and healthy.

The self-doubt chatter is what our minds do to us when we don't reach a goal. We start beating ourselves up, eroding our self-confidence and self-worth.

We cannot create healthy habits when we have low self-worth. What John says to do instead, is to get up on day one and do one pushup.

I am not kidding you. Doing one single pushup will give you a higher success rate of achieving 100 than if you tried for 100 right away. Get up on day one and do one pushup. Get up on day two and do one pushup. Get up on day three and do one pushup. Do one pushup for 30 days in a row.

Do that every single day, and every time you get up and succeed at that one pushup, your brain is saying, "Hell yes! I'm amazing." Not only is your self-worth going up, but on a mechanical level in the brain, what you are literally doing is creating neurological wiring. I think of it as a train tunnel or a tube that you're firing up. You're saying *this pathway now exists*.

The habit becomes ingrained and so well-rehearsed that the brain goes there fast. After 30 days, your brain now knows that pushups are a thing you do. You are a pushup doer.

When you get up on day 31, and you want to do two or 10 pushups, it is so much faster and easier for your brain to go there, because the wiring already exists.

I think this is incredibly fascinating. It's proven science; I'm not making up a fancy metaphor right now to help you understand. This is scientific fact. Essentially, John's message here is to *make it easy*.

It's not just a nice slogan. Making it easy is actually the best possible way for you to succeed.

The next time that you're feeling:

- Overwhelmed
- Anxious
- Like you have too much on your plate
- Like you can't possibly do what you've set out
- Doubt that you can make your dream a reality

Stop. Take a breath. Let it all out. Then, ask yourself, *how could I make this easy?* What is the simplest, smallest, tiniest step that I could take? And then ask yourself again, after you come up with that first answer. I bet there is an *even* simpler way or an even *smaller* step.

When I share these questions with my clients in our coaching sessions, we always go down at least three or four levels from that initial response.

For example, the other day, when I came up with my monumental three-part to-do list, the items were things like *finish my entire podcast production schedule.*

I could have asked myself how I could make it easier. Chunking it down, I could have decided my goal was just to finish the Monday guest interviews. That's still pretty chunky—an entire season's worth of guest interviews. How could I make it even simpler?

Even simpler: just finish writing up my show notes. Nope, that's still big—ten episodes. How could I make it even simpler? Even simpler would be *write the title for episode one and save it in a Word document.* Full stop.

You're probably freaking out right now; I know I would be if I were you. You're thinking, that's not possible, how could that be all that I do? I need to do more than that. How is that going to move me forward?

I get it. Take a deep breath and start easy.

Start simple.

I promise you, when you start with small, simple steps, and you achieve them, you are going to be on fire. That is where your fuel, your energy, and your motivation come back in, I promise you. So stick with it.

You can adopt my rule if you like it, which is that once I've done my simple, easy thing, anything else is a bonus. I'm only allowed to get *happy and excited* about those extra things I accomplish. I'm only allowed to *celebrate* my progress. There's nothing to beat myself up over after that point.

Make it easy.

Make it simple.

Repeat, repeat, repeat.

Chapter 6:

What Affirmations Are Really About

Life is about feeling good.

When I feel good, I'm a better and happier person. When I feel good, I think more clearly and have more energy.

I think back fondly on my university days. Two of my best friends were studying the same course with me. Like I mentioned in Chapter Four, we'd have these fun and productive study sessions (despite there being a lot of coffee breaks). When we'd gather together, there were particular items we'd bring with us to every one of our study sessions. We'd often be sprawled out over someone's dining room table with a multitude of textbooks and pens of various colors; I'd make sure I'd have the pink pen, the purple pen, and all the highlighters. Of course, there would be loads of cups of tea and coffee, and slabs of chocolate.

A couple of other key items would always be there. You already know about the fragranced wax melt.

The name of the fragrance would be something like "energize" or "focus" or "stress relief," and we'd have that burning in the background.

The other thing that I'd have on hand with me in the group sessions were these beautiful cards called *I Can Do It* cards by Louise Hay, a famous self-help author and teacher who is known for demonstrating how powerful affirmations can be in our lives.

Her *I Can Do It* cards are thought cards, also known as affirmation cards. Thought cards come in many variations. I have Louise Hay's *I Can Do It* deck as well as her *Power Thought* deck, which is a pack of 64 beautifully illustrated cards. Each one is thematic, and there are words on the front and back.

The phrase on the front is usually short, something along the lines of, "My life works beautifully." On the back of each card is a phrase that you can say to yourself to expand on that thought, for example, "Everything in my life works now and forevermore."

What I enjoyed back in the days of university study sessions, and what I still enjoy to this day, is that the cards are super colorful. I'm a person who enjoys color; I love bright things. During our study sessions, I'd set them on the table, and we'd all pick one and place it toward the top of our textbooks.

It was a boost every time I looked toward my card. I would read it, or it would be in my peripheral vision, and either the color sparked a little bit of joy in me, or it felt soothing and supportive to have this mantra playing in my mind. "My life works beautifully."

I'd also pick cards to support study, like, "My body is free of stress," and "I'm in balance." Whatever I needed to hear at the time, I'd have that card sitting near my books. It was a powerful tool for me personally, particularly over the peak stress period of exam time.

To prepare for exams, we'd come together even more strategically in our beautiful study group. I would pick a couple of different cards each day. I'd ask myself, *what's the message I need to hear?* I'd wake up in the morning and wonder, *what's my card?* "I trust the process of life," a card would say. "There's a rhythm and flow to life and I'm a part of it, it supports me." Just hearing those words would allow me to release some of my stress.

I want you to try an affirmation card. In a moment, I'm going to randomly pull one out for you. Even if you're thinking, *what is she on about? Not affirmation cards. They're so silly. They're just words.*

Whatever you're thinking, it doesn't really matter. The point is that the words on the card are very specifically meant to disrupt whatever is going on in your monkey mind at a point of stress, stuckness, or frustration. Chances are that the dialogue in your head is saying something that's keeping you stuck in a thought-loop. If that weren't the case, you wouldn't feel stuck. You're thinking or saying the same thing over and over to yourself. Maybe you're holding on tight to something. Maybe you're telling yourself:

- I'm not good enough.
- This isn't going to work. Or,
- What's going to happen when I fail the exam/stuff up at my project meeting/mess up the presentation?

Whatever you're telling yourself is building stress and getting you caught in a loop.

I'm finding a card for you now. Notice what happens in your body, in your mind, and in your heart as you read the following words. I've just randomly pulled one of these cards I've been playing with and shuffling while working on this chapter, and the card says, "I love my life."

There's a beautiful picture of a lady watering a sunflower; it looks gorgeous. The back says, "It is my birthright to live fully and freely. I give to life exactly what I want life to give to me. I am glad to be alive. I love life."

Now, I want you to say that out loud to yourself. If you're on the train right now, or someone's next to you, mumble it under your breath, or at least mouth it. Or write it out if you have a pen and paper. "I love my life. It is my birthright to live fully and freely. I give to life exactly what I want life to give to me. I am glad to be alive. I love life."

At the very least, what you will have noticed is the chatter in your mind has stopped. Whatever you were thinking about before is now different. The simplest thing I can say about affirmations is that they are an interruption of your train of thought. And when it comes to being busy, we need plenty of interruptions to get out of the loop. For me, it's even more powerful than that; I feel like the words float over me and actually make me feel different. When I say the words "I love my life," there's relief, certainty, and joy in that.

This is the pathway to connect you back to feeling good in your life. That's what this book is about—tapping into who you are, so that you can bring more of it out, because when you do, you feel really good.

Washing new words over you, words that hadn't previously been playing on repeat in your head, helps you to connect back into the feel-goods.

Almost eight years ago, I was somewhat newly arrived in London. It was a crossroads point in my life; I had one foot in a previous career and one foot in my new coaching career. I had a lot of questions about what that path looked like. I was also battling with a few health issues and settling into London life. As much as I was loving my new city and finding it all very vibrant, on a deeper level, my internal insight was telling me I wasn't really feeling quite myself yet. While there'd been some really positive improvements on my pathway, and some wheels were in motion, it was still pretty stressful. I didn't have much of a savings account when I moved to London. I was working whatever jobs came up at that time.

In the midst of this, I arrived home one day to find a parcel. I remember being curious because it wasn't around my birthday, and I hadn't ordered anything. I opened the parcel, and I immediately knew what it was. The box was so familiar to me. It was the *Power Thought* cards by Louise Hay. I felt a surge of energy, joy, and excitement, like I'd been connected back to myself. Like someone had brought me home again.

The cards had been an important part of my life during my university days and receiving them as a gift later played a role in connecting me back to my roots and a time when I'd felt good. The parcel arrived during what was a tumultuous time for me, and the gift became a cornerstone reminder of how sometimes I just need a simple boost, a kickstart to interrupt stressful thought patterns.

It turns out the beautiful cards in the parcel came from my gorgeous friend, Michaela. Essentially, she saw that I wasn't feeling myself. She knew all I needed was a couple of reminders to short-circuit the conversation that was going on in my head that was keeping me stuck.

You don't have to think of affirmations as a crazy, woo woo, weird, or even spiritual thing. They can be all of those things if you want them to be, but what they really are is an opportunity to surround yourself with new messages.

I use affirmation cards as a way to get into a new dialogue in my head. I use them during big crossroads in life, but also, they can be a daily practice. They sit in my drawer, and if I'm feeling a bit flat, I'll read one. They're small. They're digestible. They're pretty. They give you a boost and kickstart you into a different mental, physical, and emotional state. Sometimes the simplest things are the most powerful.

What can you do today to surround yourself with reminders so that when you are in those moments where you're clouded over and you can't see it, you have easy access to them?

Maybe you don't have a deck of cards; maybe you have a piece of paper. You can get creative and draw yourself a picture if you're very visual. You can draw it on a post-it note. You can just write one word—the one word that always makes you light up. You could write a reminder of a funny story and put it as the backdrop on your phone. These are all ways to use affirmations.

In my practice, I tend to use affirmation cards, but the purpose of affirmations, what they are really about, is to remind you to short-circuit the inner dialogue that goes on and on and keeps you stuck. Which is very powerful when it comes to freeing yourself from busy.

Chapter 7:

Getting Out of Your Head and Into Your Heart

When I first heard people say, "You just need to get in touch with your feelings," or, "You need to make decisions with your heart," there was a part of me that cringed with annoyance.

I was accustomed to using my mind to accomplish things. I was analytical, structured, and organized. These traits had served me pretty well. Whatever I'd set my mind to, I'd been able to accomplish, including doing well on my exams, choosing what university course I wanted to do, and getting a new part-time job when I needed one, or even being offered my first big career job.

Before I learned the benefits of what I'm teaching in this chapter, if someone told me to get into my heart, I'd feel annoyed because I didn't understand what they meant. It didn't make sense to me at the time.

You may relate to the feeling of enjoying achievement, being results-oriented, and liking to *make things happen*. Our ambition is a gift, giving us drive, stamina, and motivation. It's how we create things.

Yet, as with everything in life, there's also a flip side, a shadow version, of being a high achiever. If we get too caught up in our results, if we allow being in our head and being results-oriented to consume us, then it can bring us to a place of stress or inaction. Busyness kicks in to try and mask this, but really it just keeps us stuck. *Stuck* is a word that comes up time and time again in my coaching practice.

We high achievers have a particular need for control in our lives. What tends to happen is that when we've been operating in a results-oriented way for a very long time, we've also tended to operate from our heads. Our achievements and accomplishments have likely been based on a thoughtful, logical, analytical process.

If you're someone who spends a lot of time in your head, you'll know what this means. You'll instantly feel this resonating for you right now. We all have moments where we spend a lot of time in our heads. We humans are thinkers. It's how we create some of our reality.

When we're only using our head (our thoughts, our rational side of the brain) to make decisions and choices in our life, it can lead to burnout and feeling stuck, particularly if we get stuck on a thought that's not helpful.

One of my coaches shared an analogy of thinking of the rational and emotional parts of me as actors in a play. I love this metaphor because I love theater and performances. Imagine a stage; performing there is the rational part of my mind. My brain is taking center stage; it's singing and dancing. It has the lead role, it's got all the monologues, it's getting all the five-star reviews, and everyone's cheering for it. Lurking backstage, there is this other side of me. The emotional side, which I describe as the heart.

To me, the heart represents emotions and being led from an experiential, feeling space. The heart has been backstage for a while. It's capable of stepping on stage. However, rational mind has taken center stage for so long that it's become the norm for the heart to be out of the spotlight.

When you picture this stage performance happening in front of you, acknowledge that the part of you that's been front and center has some cool qualities. It can sing and dance, and it's performed pretty well up until this point. But, if you're stuck, stressed, or not getting the results you want, it could be time to consider a different act. If you want to up level, it could be time for a different show. Put another performer onstage.

What are the qualities of your heart, the emotional, feeling, sensing part of you? Surely it's got some beneficial qualities. Tap into those qualities. Tap into both the head and the heart. Imagine what kind of show or performance could play out when you're using the full cast of characters.

Moving from your head to your heart is a process of allowing yourself to get out of your thoughts, out of over-analyzing, and tapping into a place in you that is more emotional. Your heart is the part of you that is feelings-led as opposed to logic-led. And our feelings are what give us our experience of life.

Notice how different results show up in your life, or how different it feels for your day-to-day life when you are leading from your heart and allowing that part of you to take center stage.

Think about the last time you went on holiday. Maybe it was a one-day break, or maybe it was a five-week adventure. Whatever it was, I want you to pause for a moment, and think about how you decided where you wanted to go. I'm going to guess that the feeling was first for you. If you tune into that moment before you jumped into analyzing your budget and accommodation options, I'm guessing that the decision just *felt* good. Maybe you thought, *this is going to be relaxing. I just need a break.*

Now, I want you to think about the last time that you had a meal that was absolutely delicious. Maybe it was at home, and you cooked it yourself, or maybe you were out at a restaurant. How do you know that it was really delicious? What was it that made you know that?

Chances are that it was a feeling of *mmm, good*, and you probably made a decision about that meal based on how you were feeling at the time. Maybe you decided how many veggies to scoop onto your plate. Those veggies filled you up and felt really good. Maybe you perused the menu at the restaurant, and there was something about one of the items that hit a part of your body, made your mouth water, or gave you a feeling inside your heart, that prompted you to order the dish. That's a heart-led decision.

I'm purposefully giving simple examples from day-to-day life because I think often when we start to hang out in the personal growth world, and we're focused on elevating our lives and improving our results, we can think that all changes have to be *mega* changes.

If you hear someone say, "Get out of your head and into your heart," you may be thinking the decision has to be *very* emotional or *very* feelings-based.

That's a big jump to make. The fact is, there are a lot of smaller moments in life where you're probably already using your heart to make decisions. This muscle already exists for you. The process here is about noticing and strengthening your previously existing ability to move from your head to your heart.

Notice how your results feel different when you lead from your heart. Notice what felt really good about being on the holiday and making the choice for you. What felt good about the last time that you chose *you* and decided to stay in on a Friday night because you wanted to instead of going out? How did that feel different to choosing the thing that you felt like you "should" do?

Get used to acknowledging the sensation in your body when you are leading with your heart.

When I'm stuck in my head, it's because I'm seeking or craving a sense of control. Something in my life is feeling uncertain, scary, or overwhelming. Getting busy can help me feel a little more in control, because it distracts me from that uncertain feeling. I have some strategies for these times. Step one is noticing that I have gotten into a heightened state. I'm overthinking. I'm writing my pros and cons list. *Ah*, I think. *I'm here. I'm in my head right now.*

My ego, or fear-based brain, may be kicking into gear. So I say, *Thank you, ego. I get that you protect me, but I've got this. And I'm choosing something else.* This is a way of interrupting the fear-based pattern. Essentially, we are labeling what's going on. Then we can ask, *what if my heart was on center stage? What would that look like? What would that feel like? What would be different about this moment?*

It doesn't matter if you don't have an answer in that moment. The point is that you're noticing more often when your head is taking center stage.

Another strategy for getting into your heart is a simple visualization.

To listen to a free audio version of this visualization tool, go to www.FreedomFromBusy.com/gifts for an instant download. You can also do this exercise by continuing to read on from here.

Picture yourself in your head. What does it look like up there? Maybe you can see some shelves. Maybe it's really cluttered, or maybe it's really open. Maybe it's dark. Maybe it's light. Create the image with your imagination.

Then picture an elevator door. Walk over to that elevator door and push the button. The elevator opens, and you step inside. Watch and feel yourself going down, down, down.

Ding!

The door opens, you walk out, and you're in your heart space. This is the juicy part that you can play around with. As that door opens, I want you to get crystal clear on what the heart space feels and looks like. Imagine the colors and sounds there. Hang out in this space.

If you've followed along as you're reading, you may have noticed some of the warmth in your body travel down into your heart. You might notice that your head feels lighter or clearer. You might notice that something has shifted. Freeing yourself from some of the tightness of "busy". This practice is about creating a sensational shift of moving out of your head and into your heart. And once again, it's like muscle strength. The more you practice, the easier it becomes.

Throughout this book, when I share a tool, insight, or strategy, make it your own. I've spent years learning these strategies, trying them on for size, figuring out how they fit for me, and adapting them. I share them with you as a way to inspire you to come up with your own tools as well. Use what resonates most. Feel free to tailor each tool: change the size, change the color, change the shape. Do what you need to so that it feels right for you.

When you can live and lead your life from the heart space, your decisions look and feel different. When you encourage your emotional side to come out and play with your results-oriented, rational mind, everything gets up leveled. Life becomes freer.

When we get stuck in our heads, we're chasing a sense of control. We're in a fear state, stuck in a loop, going round and round in circles. The more we want control, the more out of control things feel. Stepping out of your head and into your heart space grounds you in your body, where you naturally regain control.

When you're in your heart, you have certainty. When you're in your heart, you're in a loving space for yourself. You're speaking kindly and compassionately to yourself, and everything flows from there. Remember, you've also got access to a free audio version of my 'Head to Heart' visualization tool in your additional book resources, which you can download at
www.FreedomFromBusy.com/gifts.

Chapter 8:

Why Your Emotions Matter and How to Get Okay with Them

Now that you're out of your head and in your heart, let's talk about all those feelings that may be bottled up there, in your heart.

Are you a bottler?

From the outside looking in, would anybody know if you're having a stressful day or if you cried this morning in the bathroom?

Let's undo the tight lid on that jar and explore emotions.

I want to let you know that I am a bottler. Or, at least, I *was* a bottler.

I used to appear to have it all together. I thought being strong meant not showing people my range of emotions—my happiness, sadness, stress, anxiety, all of it. If I could bottle and hide, I thought, everyone would know that they could rely on me. If I wanted to achieve—get good grades, win awards, get a great job—then my role was to be emotionally strong, which I thought meant numbing to my feelings.

I have a feeling that if you're reading this book, this part of my story resonates with you. Were you led to believe that you had to be strong and keep your feelings in check in order to achieve and become an accomplished individual?

As I grew up, I started to realize that I had a lot of emotions. I'm someone who feels a lot. I was always a very sensitive being. I would hear someone else's challenging story at school, and I would go home and feel sadness from it. Or, if someone had a cool, fun story, it would rub off on me and I'd get home from school feeling energized.

As I grew up, having a relationship with those emotions became more important. Yet, I still thought I was supposed to hold it all together. *I'm not supposed to be crying right now, I'm not supposed to be stressed, you just need to get on with it*, I would think.

Actually *getting on with it* started to become more challenging for me because of all the pushing down I was doing.

Then I began, very slowly and gradually, to change. I started to talk more about how I really felt. I began opening up to friends about how I was feeling stressed, or had a relationship issue, or family stuff going on.

I'm not really sure what the catalyst was for this shift, other than that there was too much in the jar; the lid was bursting open. I had run out of my capacity to hold it all in. And, when it started to seep out, when I did start to open up a tiny bit more, I felt better.

It was that simple. For me, this change was years in the making. I'm not saying that one morning I woke up and started to share everything. Rather, over years and years, I would share a bit more here and there. But I still wasn't fully okay with my emotions until I learned through my burnout experience in my previous career. Eventually, certain things in my life came to a tipping point; I burned out, partly due to emotional exhaustion.

From the outside looking in, it seemed that I had it all together. At work, I had multiple projects on, and my team were really busy and short-staffed, so I was taking on a lot more than I would usually have done in that position. I was also in the midst of pursuing my master's degree part-time. I had a great social life and a great home life. From the outside, it appeared that I was very busy but handling it.

But on the inside, I was not handling it.

On the inside, I was crumbling. This was partly because of the relationship I had with my emotions at the time. Interestingly enough, when I was hitting burnout, I made it really clear to my partner that I needed a release valve in my life. I'd come home crying to him every single day. That made me realize I needed a change.

One of the ideas I want to share in this book is that there are some simple things we need to know in our lives, which we aren't taught in school.

One of these is that when you talk about things, you can feel better. When you let your emotions out, you can feel better.

You may think you can hold it all together and push the pain away. You may hope that by pushing the hard feelings away or bottling them up, your pain and discomfort will be magically washed away.

That's not how it works.

Emotions are essential to experiencing life fully, instead of sleepwalking through it.

Over that particularly stressful time I just described, when I was approaching burnout, I felt like I was sleepwalking. I was numb to the emotional ups and downs that filled my life.

I would go out and have an incredible dinner with friends, but I wouldn't fully experience it. I would get a promotion at work, but I wouldn't enjoy it; it would feel like only the next thing to tick off my to-do list. There was no taking in the feeling of that experience, even the good stuff, because I was so busy trying to hold down the uncomfortable and stressful feelings.

Life is to be experienced. We're here on this beautiful planet to *experience* it. To *feel* it. To journey through it. Part of the meaning of life is to actually *feel it*.

Our emotions are how we feel and experience things. So, why would we want to numb them? Because we think it will make the difficult emotions go away. Our brains are wired to keep us safe. They will try to keep us away from pain or discomfort or anything that equals challenge to our life. But, when we numb our pain, we also numb our joy. When we numb the uncomfortable stuff, we numb some of the happiness as well.

Most Friday nights leading up to my burnout experience, I'd go out for beautiful group dinners with a great group of friends. We'd have incredibly fun nights, and I'd wake up on Saturday mornings and not really remember them. This was not because we had a wild, revelrous night, but because I was only half there. I wasn't fully present. When I think back to those memories now, I can't fully embody them because I was holding back on myself. I didn't fully experience all of the joy and incredible highs and lows of that time; I was numbing out.

Brené Brown says, "We cannot selectively numb emotions. When we numb the painful emotions, we also numb the positive emotions."

During this stressful time in my life that I've been describing, the more I opened up, the better I felt emotionally. I felt better in my body, too. I had quite a few physical symptoms of my stress at the time, including migraines. The further I went on the path of opening up to my emotions, the better I felt mentally, physically, and emotionally.

The more under pressure your body is from emotional stress, the more frequently you'll experience colds. You'll also be more susceptible to anxiety, insomnia, and other illnesses.

When you can start to see your mind-body connection, you can also understand that your emotions are just as critical to your experience of life as your physical wellbeing and mental health.

How much more wellness and vitality could you bring into your life by experiencing and taking care of your full emotional spectrum?

Once you allow yourself to feel exactly where you are, you can move up on the emotional spectrum. You can do this by following an emotional guidance scale. One emotional scale I like is from Abraham-Hicks; I first heard about the scale through Gabrielle Bernstein.

I want you to imagine the scale as a beautiful rainbow. Every emotion on the rainbow has a different charge. It can either energize you or drain you a little bit more or less. The scale isn't about only staying in a high-energy, super-charged, ridiculously happy, over-positive state. It's about knowing that you have access to all the different emotions.

Let's say you're stuck in a funk. You're feeling anger, frustration, or irritation. The point is not to leap over a bunch of other feelings and arrive at happiness and joy. The point is inching a bit closer to feeling better. How could you take just a tiny nudge toward happiness and joy? The next emotion up from frustration on the Abraham-Hicks emotional guidance scale is pessimism. Can you move from frustration to pessimism? One notch up from pessimism is boredom. And one more notch up, and you've arrived at contentment.

If you're not allowing yourself to even know that you're at a point of anger, frustration, or irritation, there's no way to climb toward the higher state, feel-good emotions. *You must recognize where you are to begin with.* All your emotions are a gift. Each is part of a beautiful rainbow.

Here's a simple and powerful practice to develop a loving relationship with your emotions. Simply acknowledge their beauty and worth instead of pushing them away. Invite your negative emotions in for a few moments.

Now, I know you're probably squirming in your chair right now. You're saying, "I don't want the anger, I don't want the frustration, I don't want to *be here*, Danielle! I'm reading this book so that I can bring more joy into my life! I want to create change. I want things to be different. I don't want the stress. I don't want the crankiness."

And I get it. All I'm inviting you to do with this simple practice is to acknowledge where you are right now. If you're stuck in a pattern of pushing away your draining emotions, that is a numbing out technique. You may be numbing your pain, but it also means you're not going to get to joy. You're not going to get to any of the things that I've been talking about in this book if you're numbing out to where you are right now.

I want you to experience the full scale. I want you to know what it's like to be on any one of the beautiful colors in the rainbow. When you can acknowledge each feeling and welcome it in, I promise you that you'll be able to move on from it as well.

First acknowledge, then allow.

Acknowledge.

Allow.

Adopt this as a mini mantra in your life every time you feel yourself tensing, pushing away, and trying not to feel. *Acknowledge and allow.*

Acknowledge can look like naming the emotion; that helps me. Label it as stress or whatever it is.

I'm really stressed. This is pain. I feel really sad right now.

Try this, and notice what happens when you acknowledge, name, and allow it. As you practice this over time, you'll notice that there's a moment of release, like a gentle, easy sigh. Like you're giving yourself a hug. *It's okay to feel this. This is valid.*

You'll also notice how much more quickly, smoothly, elegantly, and gracefully the negative emotion moves on. It extinguishes, settles, or gets absorbed. You then have space to move on to a better feeling emotion.

Acknowledge and allow gives you back the spice of life. Try it and get access to all of the colors of the rainbow.

I want to celebrate your progress with this book. We're about halfway through. You've reached a pivotal lesson: having a relationship with your emotions will bring you a fullness of life. Like I said in the beginning, please feel free to get in touch about this or any chapter. Let me know what colors in the rainbow you're experiencing today.

Chapter 9:

How to Not Get Swept Up in Others' Emotions

Here's a question that comes up in a few different ways as I'm working with my clients:

How do I avoid getting swept up by other people's negative emotions?

Let's say your colleagues are moaning about something. How do you not let *their* pain or discomfort derail how you're doing in *your* life?

Avoiding emotional derailment is a powerful and important skill to have, especially for someone who is super sensitive.

I have been highly sensitive ever since I was little. But, as you probably picked up from the last chapter, I never really knew it until I hit burnout. Recently, I've been learning about the concept of being an empath and identifying with parts of it. An empath is someone who feels things really deeply.

For me, for example, I'll see an old lady struggling up the stairs at the train station and feel sadness and a yearning to help her. I'll often walk away with that feeling—it will stick.

My partner knows me well, but once in a while, he'll jokingly ask why we can never watch any drama shows together. He knows I'll get upset; I get really wrapped up in drama. I think about some of the drama shows I would watch through my university years. I'd bawl my eyes out afterward and go to bed thinking about all the characters and wondering how they resolved their problems. I would know it was just a TV show, but the emotion still latched onto me.

Now, I protect my emotional equilibrium. When I sit down to watch TV, I like a good rom-com or a comedy with a happy ending. I absorb a lot of emotion and energy throughout my day, and when it comes down to chilling in front of the TV, I don't need too much drama.

Not getting swept up in the emotions of others is not to be mistaken with not wanting *any* emotions. Rather, we're talking about staying within your own sphere of emotional influence and not allowing yourself to absorb other people's emotions to the extent that they dilute your own positive emotions or derail you completely.

Do you come home at the end of the workday not just feeling exhausted because of what's going on for *you*, but also because of:

- The conversations that you've been having at work?
- Thinking of a person who's really stressed and has no idea how they are going to handle their problems?
- Wondering if it's okay that another colleague didn't finish a project on their deadline and holding onto the fact that they were really upset over it?
- Listening to someone else vent and complain and realizing that *you* now feel de-energized and grumpy?

This pattern of absorbing what's going on around us adds to our busyness, and often without us even realizing it.

If you answered yes to any of the above questions, the following points are for you.

The first point that I want to make is that it's perfectly okay to feel how you feel. Coming home having taken on other people's emotions doesn't make you a bad person. There's no right or wrong way to feel. We're all sensitive beings.

The second point is to notice and pay attention to how you're feeling throughout your day *and* at the end of the day. Do a mini stock-take with yourself. Practice awareness, and you'll start to notice themes. You might think, *I had a really good day, so why do I feel like shit right now?* That observation could give you an indication that you might be owning someone else's emotion. Maybe you're loving your job and home life at the moment, but you had a conversation on the phone this morning and you're still feeling grumpy, irritated, or off from it. Take stock with yourself a little more regularly. Check in with yourself: *How am I feeling right now, and what does this relate to? Is it related to me, or is it related to someone else?*

This brings me to my third point, which is to let go of that which you can't control. If a feeling isn't related to you, if you can't find any evidence or reason for a feeling going on inside of you, then it might not be yours. And if it's not your feeling, it's not under your control. You may be carrying around a bit of someone else's grumpiness, for example. While you can empathize with that person's experience, acknowledge them, and hold space for them, their emotions are not yours to *own*. Their emotions are also not something you can control. A lot of the time, when we're holding onto an emotion for someone else, it's because we want it resolved. We want them to feel good. We want to fix it.

Let's think about my example of seeing the elderly lady struggling up the stairs at the train station. What I'm really doing is projecting my fear. I'm assuming that she must feel bad. The truth is, I don't know how she feels. She might be feeling incredible. Who am I to define her experience? I'm *assuming* that she must feel bad, and I'm owning that bad feeling. Now, that's not serving her, and it's not serving me. It also isn't something that I can control.

There are things you can control, and things you can't control. You *can't* control someone else's experience of their life. You *can't* control someone else's emotions and energy. Center yourself on what *is* in your control. This is not always easy. I know what it feels like to *really* want to make someone feel better. It's hard to watch people in discomfort or pain. But there's a reason they're having the experience they're having. When empathizing, make a clear distinction between trying to control their emotions and being truly supportive by listening, holding space, and sending loving attention toward them.

Something that helps me is to bring love into the conversation inside my head. I might think, *there's a lady struggling up the stairs. I wonder if she's feeling discomfort. How can I bring some love to that?* Sometimes that could literally look like some support, as in walking over and saying, "Excuse me, do you want some help up the stairs?" Sometimes it could mean only thinking loving thoughts. Maybe someone else went to help the lady up the stairs. I might send love and gratitude to both of them by picturing loving thoughts and feelings flowing toward them.

When we allow ourselves to go to a feeling of love more often, it becomes more easily accessible to us as a response to difficult situations.

If you find yourself with negative emotion clinging to you, or you want to control or fix things for someone else, ask, "How could I switch this to love?" Saying the word *love* will flip you into thinking a little bit differently, and that could be all you need.

My fourth and final point on this topic is around boundaries. If others are being negative around you, if they're talking about things you don't want to talk about, or if they are whining and moaning all the time, how do you not let that ruin how you're feeling all day or pull you into a slump?

You need to create a boundary in this situation. It could be something as simple as saying to those people in your life, "Thank you for sharing. Right now, I'm practicing restoring my energy, and I've noticed that conversations like this feel a little draining, or triggering, or too much for me. Can we change the topic?"

You could also create a physical boundary. You could say, "I don't want to be part of this conversation," and then physically remove yourself by walking away.

It's perfectly okay for you to create your own boundaries. It is okay to know what feels good to you, what doesn't feel good to you, and to speak up about it.

At the time of this writing, we are under certain restrictions due to the Covid-19 global pandemic. There's a lot of heaviness and negativity in the news, as you can imagine. I'm very selective about how I absorb information; I like to take in factual information straight from the source. I studied economics and have worked in government policy and for health charities; this background has trained me to be great at distilling complex information and going directly to the source. This way, I can avoid getting mixed information through all the various news and social media channels. Getting my news second-hand is just not something that works for me personally. It doesn't make me feel good; it drains me, and that means I cannot be in the strong and supportive space I need to be in for myself and for others in my life. And, it's another way "busy" can show up, if I'm not intentional in my approach.

My partner is someone who loves news and media information. His brains works very differently than mine; he needs a lot of detail and information in his life. And that's beautiful. It's how he absorbs things and how he makes sense of the world. While that's amazing for him, it's not something that works for me. So I've created a boundary around that with him. I've said to him, lovingly, "This is how I'm approaching things because this works for me; this is what feels good for me. I would ask that before you share a piece of news with me, you check that it's okay." This boundary has been great because he either just won't share that information or he'll check if I want to hear it, or he'll start to share, and I'll say, "Do you mind just pausing for a moment, and checking if this something that I need to hear right now because I'm filtering what I take in."

Bottom line? What feels good to you is the *most* important thing. When you're in a place of what feels good to you, you are grounded and secure; your nervous system knows that you are safe, and you are more capable of handling challenging situations. You're able to access your own sustainable fuel source for energy, motivation, and clarity about your decisions. Boundaries are incredible. Speak up for what is okay for you, and what's not okay for you.

If you're not sure what your boundaries are, start by answering this question in your journal:

What is okay and what is not okay?

It's based on my favorite definition of boundaries, from Brene Brown, "making clear what's okay and what's not okay, and why."

This journal prompt is a simple way to clarify your own boundaries and keep yourself from getting swept up in negative emotions that don't belong to you—freeing yourself from busy in the process.

Chapter 10:

Figuring Out What Lights You Up

My older sisters were dancers and gymnasts. I grew up watching them perform.

Being the youngest, with three older sisters, there was always this sense of excitement and adventure for me when I'd get to go and watch one of them perform. With all the rehearsing going on in the house, there'd be a feeling of build-up toward the big event. I'd get all dressed up and go along with my parents to watch the show.

Something magical used to happen for me, in part because I got to watch my sisters in a different role. I got to watch them bring a new scene to life. And also, because anytime I stepped inside a theater or a place with a stage and people performing, something in my body used to come alive.

Let's fast-track to when I was a bit older and could engage in activities of my choosing. I was always drawn to speech and drama; I loved performing. I really enjoyed watching musicals on TV. There was something that fascinated me around people transforming into new characters, bringing out this incredible side of them that you might not know even existed if you were just chatting to them. I used to just sit in stunned awe of people's voices. I loved chorus numbers.

One of my favorite musicals of all time is *Chicago*, because of the individuality of each of the characters, the stories they all have, and how they come together and perform chorus line numbers. When I'd see a performance of *Chicago* or any musical like it, my heart would start thumping; my foot would start tapping. I felt like I was part of the show.

I'm sure there is something in your life where you have a similar sense, where your body starts to come alive. Maybe it's not speech, drama, or theater. Maybe it's something else like being on a tennis court or opening up your favorite book and curling up on the couch. We all have associations where we notice that a place inside of us buzzes. We come alive and feel lit up.

On any journey I'd ever taken, including a trip to New York and a trip to London before moving here, my priority was always to go to the theater. There was always something about being at a live performance that enveloped my whole being and made me feel like I was up there, on the stage with the performers, transported to this whole other world. It was really magical for me. I had a feeling that I belonged there in that space.

Now, fast forward to my having moved to London and having lived here for almost eight years at the time of this writing. As I created this dream of living in London and began bringing it into reality, part of my dream was getting to go to theater shows and performances that light me up. I saw myself living in London and going to jazz bars and musicals. Before I started putting the steps in place to make the London dream happen, I would visualize attending all the shows, and it would stir up all of these emotions inside me as I pictured myself seated in the grand theaters, immersed in the beautiful performances.

A couple years ago, I'd gone through a period when, between myself and my partner, there were lots of things happening in our business lives and our personal lives. Our schedules felt full. I began to notice that every single day, I'd be out in central London, seeing these posters for theater shows, and I'd always take note, thinking, *I must go see that. And that. And that.*

I realized one morning as I was looking at all these posters that it had been a very long time since I'd seen a show. I'd been telling myself, *I'll do that when…*

…it's my birthday.

...so-and-so comes to visit.

...I finish this project.

...my partner and I have wrapped up loose ends on this other project.

Is there something in your life where you're telling yourself the same thing? *I'll do that when...*

Maybe what you want to do is something that you know intrinsically is something that you love, that makes you come alive. Yet there's a dialogue in your head that says, *not now. I'll do it when...*

When does *when* arrive? Does it ever?

I realized I'd gone a few *years* of not prioritizing going to the theater. Of course, there were lots of reasons for that. However, what I noticed in that moment of realization, going up an escalator, watching all these posters of shows that I really wanted to see go by, was that a voice in my head piped up. It said, "Part of the reason you moved to London, part of your dream, part of what makes you truly come alive, is the theater, and being here to experience it first-hand. You're in one of the most magical cities in the world when it comes to theater. You're able to access it ridiculously easily. What is stopping you?"

For what purpose would I stop myself from going to the theater?

Now of course, lots of reasons, which are really just excuses, came up. Beautifully wrapped up, well-presented excuses, but excuses, nonetheless. I would tell myself I didn't have enough money. That my diary was too full. That I should wait until there was a better reason. That I couldn't possibly just go by myself. That it would mean taking some time off of work. I could go on and on. You can see how tempting it is to use "busy" as the reason why something hasn't happened in our lives.

However, I also know that the only way to create what you want in your life, to feel the way you want to feel, is to create it for yourself.

You have a choice. How you feel is your responsibility; no one else can make you feel a certain way. That feeling you want is initiated in *your* body, heart, and soul. You make the choice. There are many small moments in our life where we can take more responsibility for how we're feeling.

I wasn't taking responsibility for doing what I wanted to do. I wasn't paying enough attention to those things in my life that really made me come alive.

I decided in that particular moment on the escalator that all of my excuses were things I could come up with solutions for. I could book the cheapest seats. I could book months in advance. I could make a commitment and put it in my diary so that when it came up, it was a must. It was just there, and it just happened.

And I did just that.

I started to prioritize it; when I would see a poster, I would book the show, whether it was one week away or six months away. It wasn't on my to-do list; I would just do it because I prioritized it.

What started to happen naturally is since that time a couple of years ago, every month or two, there has been a show in my life. (At least until the global pandemic changes in 2020. I can't wait to get back to regular theater!)

I felt such joy looking forward to the shows I had pre-booked. Even while booking the ticket, feelings of excitement and anticipation would wash over me. Then show day would arrive. Those moments of opening up the theater doors, finding my seat, the lights dimming, and the stage curtains opening would make me come alive. Whatever excuse or reason that I had come up with before no longer mattered. Being there in that moment was worth overcoming my excuses a million times over.

When we prioritize joy, we prioritize those things that make us come alive.

Maybe one of those things for you is an experience like going to the theater. Maybe it's something as simple as sipping your cup of tea while it's still warm instead of letting it get cool on the counter as you're rushing around. It's about finding those things, those moments, those experiences, that make you come alive, and prioritizing them. This will have a ripple effect throughout your entire life.

When I prioritize the things that bring me joy, I'm putting myself first. When I put myself first, I actually get excited and energized. I'm more joyful when my partner walks through the door at the end of the day, and I'm able to be more present with him. I'm able to be more loving to people in my life. Any resentful energy I would have had dissipates. I feel lighter and freer when I'm choosing to take responsibility for how I create joy in my life. I get to feel the way *I want* to feel.

This doesn't mean I get to wipe my slate clean and never experience anything challenging again. What it *does* mean is that how I choose to show up in more challenging moments comes from a full tank of my best energy. I can come from a place of calm, peacefulness, and a bit more joy, maybe the moment before or the day before or the week before. Overall,

I have more resilience to handle whatever comes my way.

My invitation to you is to notice, what are those things in *your* life that light you up? What are the things that make you come alive, get your heart pounding, your eyes sparkling, and your energy buzzing? Maybe they're really small things. Maybe they're huge things. Whatever your things are, I want you to write them down and then begin to notice and pay attention to them. Take 30 seconds to ask yourself: Where in my life am I prioritizing this activity? Where in my life am I not prioritizing this? Where in my life could I welcome more of this?

I promise you, when you do, that is where the ripple of change takes shape. When you do feel that buzz, that heart pounding more often, when you choose joy more often, then the challenges, the problems, the things that you're really stuck on or fuzzy on or don't have clarity on right now, those things will unlock in a profound way.

Chapter 11:

The Simple Shift That'll Give You Back Control

Do you have moments where you feel like your world is spinning?

Overwhelm is a word that I hear a lot and that I can really relate to.

Sometimes I get myself in a tizz. I used to really let overwhelm unhinge me; it would almost feel like my body was boiling and overflowing with tense energy.

I'm not alone in having a panic response to overwhelm. We start to reach for things to plug the hole and fix it. We tend to leak a lot of energy because we start to focus on things that aren't going to move us forward or give us results.

At home in overwhelm, you may find that you're crankier with your partner or loved ones. At work, you may find you start to miss things, forget about emails, or make silly mistakes along the way. All these little things start to add to the tension until everything feels out of control. It's usually also where we turn to *busyness*.

I believe all human beings are control freaks. When we go into overwhelm and stress, we are craving getting our sense of control back. To think of it in a more resourceful way, the element of control we're craving is more so a sense of certainty, comfort, and safety. This desire is pretty natural, considering how our brain is wired to keep us safe.

There's something that drives things to get even worse when you're going through overwhelming or stressful moments or phases in your life. And it's this, when you are having a particularly stressful time, you are likely focusing on *fixing things externally to feel better*.

What tends to happen if we've had a crisis or stressful experience is that we try to resolve things from the outside. We try, for example, to tell our boss that they're doing things wrong. We get grumpy with our external stakeholders. Or we decide that our friends are in a really stressful mood and we don't want to hang out with them anymore. We try to fix our partner's flaws.

Everything seems like an external problem to be fixed. If I could just get my friend to call me back, then everything would be okay. If I could just get my boss to move that deadline, then everything would be fine. If my boss just went on holidays and came back happy and relaxed, then that would make my life better, and then I'd want to stay on in this job.

We come up with unwritten, hidden rules for ourselves. If *this* happens, then I can be okay. If *that* happens, then I can relax. If I can just tick off everything on my to-do list, then I will feel back in control again.

Part of that process means we're focusing on changing something *external* to us to make ourselves feel better. A lot of the time, if not *all* of the time, external things are out of our control.

Here's a partial list of things we don't have control over:

- The weather
- Our best friend's mood
- Whether our boss slept for eight hours or not last night
- Whether the trains get delayed in the morning
- Whether your favorite restaurant runs out of your favorite meal

These are things that are external to us. Yet when stuck on overwhelm and stress, we tend to focus on trying to fix these things even though they are out of our control.

There is a simple shift you can make to help you feel better and ultimately *more* in control of your life.

Start to notice what you are focusing on controlling or changing. What would happen if you started to focus on things that are actually in your control? Here's what I know to be true:

What you do have control over is you.

You have control over how you feel about the train running late. You have control over how you choose to respond to your boss's cranky mood because they didn't sleep much the night before. You have control over your reactions, the words that come out of your mouth, the thoughts that you create, and the feelings that you generate. Knowing that in itself gives certainty and comfort. Knowing that you always have a choice over how you choose to feel and respond gives you back your sense of control.

I call this choice theory. When I know that I have a choice, then everything else becomes easier. One of my favorite equations that I draw up for my clients is:

Event + Response = Outcome

This is a popular concept in management, leadership, entrepreneurship, personal development spheres and more. And I've seen it referred to in all sorts of places, because of its simplicity to remember and its power to transform.

The thing that happens, plus your response, equals the result. You don't have control over the event. You don't have control over someone else's mood, the restaurant's meal plan, the train, or public transport schedules. Those things are the event. You *do* have control over your response: how you show up in that situation, what you choose to think about, and what you make it mean. There are two parts of this equation, and while you don't have any control over the first bit, you do have a lot of control over the second bit, which naturally means the result, the output, has to change.

So, if you want something to change in your life, you *could* keep complaining about the situation. You could say, "Oh, my God, I work in such a stressful environment. This project just keeps going on and on and on. My boss never appreciates me."

Or you could make another choice. Choice theory would say that you could start to take responsibility for your results. You could start to take responsibility for what happens after the equals sign. Freedom from busy comes from paying attention to your *response*.

How do you go about doing that?

Here's an example. Before I went full time in my current business, I had a job that was based on my previous career path. I'd grown into my previous career over many years and it was something that I was very good at, and I did actually enjoy *some* of the process of the job. But the thing I didn't like about the job was that it wasn't my dream. My heart was set on another dream. I knew what the dream was, and I needed to bring it to life. When I was in this old job, there were lots of pressures, strains, and stresses, not only because there were lots of projects going on, but because every day my internal rhetoric was *why am I here?*

That was the mindset I was in and it was causing me a lot stress. I'd rock up at work every day thinking, I don't want to be here. I want to be working on my business. I want to be growing my dream. I want to be coaching more. Why am I pouring more time and energy into a career path that I know is not going anywhere?

On top of that, it was a stressful job in itself. There would be problems with the project. There would be real stumbling blocks to get over and challenging conversations to have. At the same time, I was also studying part-time to get my coaching qualification. I was learning all about growing a business and starting to put wheels in motion to bring it to life, so it was almost like I was working two jobs.

There was this moment one day, on my way to work, when I could see clearly that I was heading down the same path as I'd been on in my previous career when I'd burned out. I was taking on a lot of things, and I was allowing them to take over me. I had this moment of realizing *this is a choice. I could leave the job today. Nobody is telling me to stay. I am choosing to be here because I want to be here. I want the security.*

I also really enjoyed the company of the people around me. I was good at the project and enjoying the progress I was making. In that moment I realized that *hang on a second, I have a big decision to make here.* I have a choice. I could choose to keep rocking up in the office and complaining that I don't want to be in this job; I want to go do the business. I can keep complaining about how I'm not there yet, and I wish I were there. Or I could acknowledge that showing up here on the job is a choice. I've chosen to be here, so how do I want to feel being here each day?

And it was a pretty big decision that actually changed everything for me.

Saying to myself, *I'm choosing to be here* was a big release. Pressure was off my shoulders. I suddenly took on the attitude of, *well, if I'm choosing to be here, I can enjoy this. This can be fun.*

I could enjoy the process. I could be grateful every morning. I had an amazing job to go to. My team were incredible. I really valued their minds, their creativity, and their company. I had full ownership of a project, and that felt really good to me because I was putting my years of experience into practice to add value.

Everything changed from that moment on because I took ownership. I took full responsibility for the part of the equation that I had control over, instead of focusing on the part of the equation that I didn't have control over. I didn't have control over everyone else's project deadlines, everyone else's moods, the culture of the organization, or the culture of external stakeholders.

I shifted my focus onto what I could control, which for me at the time was my response to my situation and my circumstances. From that moment onward, it became easier, despite having a very full schedule. People at the time would ask me, "How are you studying and having clients and growing your business while you've got all this busy and stressful project stuff going on?" I'd say, "I'm choosing to have some fun along the way and allowing it to flow in whatever way it needs to."

About 12 months later, I transitioned into my business full time and resigned from that job. I wouldn't have had nearly as stress-free a transition, nor gotten the results that I wanted, either in my day job, or my business, and had fun at the same time at my job, if I hadn't made that choice.

Choice theory is an essential tool to have in your kit. Know that this exists at all times. If you want your life to be a certain way, if you want to feel a certain way, if you don't want the stress anymore, then you can invite yourself to take more responsibility for your life. Choice theory has the power to give you back your sense of control, which is the thing that you're craving when you're in an overwhelm—and busy—spin.

Next time that you're stuck, next time that you feel that that pressure building, I want you to try to shift your attention to what is in your control: how you're choosing to respond to the situation.

Ask yourself:

- What choice would I like to make right now?
- What response am I choosing right now?
- What could I choose to do differently?

Take full responsibility for your results by choosing your response, which is the only thing you truly have control over.

This is a challenging habit to start, but it's rewarding and fulfilling, because it puts you back in the driver's seat. It feels incredible to know that results, happiness, success, and accomplishments, as well as any joy that you're creating in your life, can actually be generated from you.

Chapter 12:

The Thing That's Stopping Your Joy

I've led over 100 hours of group workshops.

Most of them were on the theme of ditching stress and creating more balance in life. *Balance* is a word that gets thrown around a lot. It's something most of us can imagine we want.

The first question I asked at every single one of these workshops would leave the room fairly stunned and silent. It's a really simple question that can unlock so much and give us what we want. Yet so many people don't ask it of themselves.

A lot of the people that would end up in my workshop rooms were really busy. They were either in high-flying careers, or managing a lot of responsibilities at home, or both. They were feeling stressed and on the road to burnout. They wanted to create more balance in their lives. Yet, when I asked the question I will share with you in a moment, they became confused or would say, "I don't know, actually."

When there's something you want to create in your life—maybe balance, joy, presence, spaciousness, less stress, more money, or a different job, whatever it is—so often, the reason that we know we want to create that is we're really clear on the *problems* we have.

We're clear that we *don't* want stress. For example, we might imagine our problems vividly and say, "I don't want the pressure. I don't want the running around. I don't want to go to bed late every night. I don't want to have to get up at the crack of dawn. I don't want to be on the train when it's rush hour."

Yet, when we haven't spent any time asking ourselves what we *do* want, we tend to get stuck in a spiral of *I don't want **this** anymore*. This drains us because we keep repeating over and over what we don't want, but we don't have any clarity, or a pathway forward, because we haven't even stopped to ask what we **do** want.

So, in my balance workshops, I'd take people through a formula for creating more balance. We'd start with this very simple question. You've probably guessed what it is by now:

What do you want?

Before you rattle off what you think you want or don't want, you have to stop. Pause and give yourself time and space to consider your answer to this question. Define what it is *you* want.

In the context of my balance workshops, I would ask my participants:

- What exactly does *balance* mean to you?
- How will you know when you have it?

Simple, right? Yet, if I asked you to try and answer that right now in the context of what you're trying to create or change in your life, do you have an answer? Do you have a really clear picture of what you *do* want? And as you answer, I want you to be really conscious of the language you choose. For example, notice when you go to what you *don't* want. When you say, "Well, what I want is to not feel so stressed. What I want is to stop being so busy all the time," I'd like you to flag that.

Leading from a place of joy means you have to know what joy's about. It means you have to have a sense of why it matters to you in the first place.

There is plenty of scientific research around why it's important to be in a joy state, to be in a balanced state within our body, our mind, our soul, and how that generates incredible benefits in our life, including to our health and wellbeing. However, if you don't know what *it* is to begin with, you're not going to get *it*. If you don't know what *it* means to you, you're not going to create any shifts. You're going to stay stuck where you are.

Another reason why this question is critical, and why I spend a lot of time on it in my workshops, is that every single person is different. There are lots of big, beautiful words that we use all of the time when talking about what we desire. We talk about balance, success, achievement, and even abundance. But every single person is going to have a different feeling and connotation of what a particular word means to them. Regardless of whether you look up the dictionary definition, everyone even reading that definition will conjure up a different image in their mind and a different feeling in their body. For this reason, I can't answer this question for you. I can't tell you what joy or balance is for you, personally.

I interviewed Nancy Jane Smith, author of *The Happier Approach* and specialist in working with 'High Functioning Anxiety' for my podcast last year. We had a discussion around why it's so important to create more of our own language around words like joy, happiness, and balance. We were talking about the distinction between joy and happiness, which was cool because it was something that I hadn't personally thought of in my own life.

If *you* don't know what "joy," "happiness," or "balance" is for you, you can't have it. Which is why it is so important to create the spaciousness for yourself to actually consider this.

Before you say, "I don't know," let me tell you a little secret. This is something that happens in all of my coaching sessions. When I hear, "I don't know," I get so excited. I celebrate it. I'm jumping up and down for my beautiful clients because "I don't know" means they're up against the edge of this incredible growth zone.

Are you saying *I don't know*? If so, you are about to go somewhere you have never been before. Hold that space for yourself. Stay with the "I don't know," and ask yourself, "What if I *did* know?" Then pause there for a moment. I promise you, there are beautiful answers within you if you allow yourself to linger.

If you don't recognize it, if you can't describe it, if you can't get crystal clear on what it means to you, then it could have been there the whole time to access, and you wouldn't have even known.

So, if joy, or even balance, is something that you want to create more of in your life, if you know that you spend too much time in stress, busyness, and overwhelm, if you know that you want to be more present in your relationships, show up more for friends, or simply want to have some space for yourself to sit on the couch on a Friday night; what if that which you are craving, that *feeling* that you get from sitting on the couch, that *feeling* of being present in your relationships, what if it was already in your life? What if it is already there, but because you haven't taken the time to define it, to know what it looks like and feels like, you've been dismissing it the whole time?

That's what we end up doing when we're only chasing what we *don't* want. If you want to feel differently, then you have to know what that change means for you.

Here's what joy means for me. For me, when I think about joy, I think about so many things. Joy to me is ease in my body. Joy to me feels like I am light and untouchable and powerful. Joy to me feels like a warm hug on the inside. Joy to me is sitting alone at a coffee shop with my notebook. Joy to me is calling a girlfriend and leaving a voice note telling her how much I love her. Joy to me is seeing the smile on one of my loved ones' faces, and particularly my nieces and nephews, and seeing them laugh over something really silly. Joy to me is seeing a big, bright, bunch of beautiful flowers, even if I'm not bringing them home for myself. It's me, fully grounded in myself.

For me, what those moments give is this feeling of energy, charge, and power. When I have that energy, charge, and power, my body, mind, and soul feel aligned. My thoughts change. After I've seen a bunch of beautiful flowers, for example, I can feel a shift happen. I'm more energized. I make better decisions. And my life lights up in ways I couldn't even imagine before.

I want you to be able to get to the point where you can tune into those magnificent moments, whatever they are for you. Yet if you haven't defined joy for yourself, you're not going to be able to notice how much more energized you are when those moments happen, and you're not going to be able to translate that into better decisions. You're not going to be able to channel that energy into getting a project done so you can get home earlier, or whatever it is you want.

Here's the invitation in this chapter:

Define what you *want*.

Maybe your word is on this list:

- Joy
- Happiness
- Success
- Peace
- Calm
- Balance

Find a word that really resonates for you. You'll know—you'll have already had that word jump out at you while reading this chapter. Maybe it's one of the words I shared above, or maybe not. Trust your first instinct. Write that word down on a piece of paper. And ask yourself, *what does this mean to me?*

How would you define it? If someone asked you, "What does that word mean?" How could you bring it to life for them? If you were drawing a picture of it or describing it in sounds, or in feelings, what would you say or do? I want you to give it lots of color. Keep coming back to it. Pull out a blank piece of paper, write the word on it, and every time you get an "I don't know," I want you to sit with it and stretch that silence a little longer, and ask, "What if I did know?

Notice what starts pouring out of you and commit that to paper. Maybe it means that you come back to that piece of paper multiple times over the course of an entire week or month. Maybe you just sit down for five minutes, and you notice it rolls out of you. Know that it can shift over time because life is an evolution, and that's what it's all about. Once you bring your word to life, you're going to notice how much more of it already exists in your life. When you are noticing what you already have, and all the joy already around you, you can magnify it and create even more of that which you want.

The technique I've shared in this chapter is game-changing. I know it sounds simple. Yet you probably haven't done it yet. Before you think, *this is too easy, it couldn't possibly make a difference,* give it a go and see what unfolds.

Chapter 13:

How to Build Confidence in Yourself

Confidence is a feeling of certainty in yourself.

When you know what you want, you're able to speak up about it, and when you can move through life with a sense of clarity, you have confidence. Confidence is not a skill set that you put on your resume. It's not about being good at public speaking. Confidence oozes from deep within. It's not necessarily about the tasks that someone can complete.

If you've ever felt lacking in confidence in an area of your life, then you probably could just as easily think about a time when you *did* feel confident. Think back to the very last time you felt really confident.

Here's an example from my life: I'm really confident when I'm at home with my partner. With him, I'm completely myself, and I have certainty in myself. I have no problem telling him my opinion, sticking to my boundaries, or saying what I need, whether it's alone time, together time, or anything else. My sense of confidence is coming from deep within. I also feel confident in the work that I do in the world. It's coming from a place of having a message to share, personal experience, and knowing what I'm talking about is from deep within me.

Someone in my Joy Club recently asked me, "How can I build confidence in myself?" My answer anytime I get this question always comes down to asking, "How can you feel more certain about *you*? How can you feel more certain about how you're showing up and about what you really want in the world?"

When we have a sense of certainty in *ourselves,* we make decisions quickly and easily. I have no problem making a decision about what I want to eat for dinner because I know my likes and dislikes. I know what mood I'm in. That's confidence. That's certainty.

Imagine how it would be if you showed up in all areas of your life with this kind of certainty. The decisions just happen. Imagine it at work. There, you can probably think of moments where you have felt more confident and less confident. In the moments that you felt really confident, what was happening with how you were making decisions? Was it happening automatically? Were you stopping to ask a bunch of people for their opinions? Or were you just getting on with things? How did you approach a project where you felt really confident?

Now contrast your answers with how you might approach a project where you do not feel confident. Maybe you ask more questions, or fewer. Maybe you retreat a little, or perhaps you speak up more because you want to be seen to be confident. We all have different ways we approach times we lack confidence. What I want you to notice when you're answering the questions I'm throwing out right now is what the difference is between times when *you personally* feel more confident versus less confident. In these scenarios, there's going to be a difference in:

- How you make decisions.
- How much or how little you know what you want.
- Your sense of clarity.
- How you're feeling on the inside.

Once again, we come back to feelings. You may have noticed that this is a book about feeling all of your feelings. If confidence is something you want to focus on feeling more of, that starts with getting to know how you feel in all of these situations. More specifically, I want you to start with *certainty* in yourself. What makes you feel really certain? What gives you a sense of *I've got this*? What do you just know without hesitation? And how does it make you feel when you know those things?

I'll give some purposefully small examples. Finding micro-moment examples in our lives helps us pay attention and start spotting the bigger ones that can go unnoticed because they're deeply automatic. For me, I feel really certain about the flavors of chocolate I love. One is butterscotch, and the other is sea salt. I know I love these. If someone asks me if I want the mint chocolate, I immediately can feel a level of certainty in my body that it's a no; it feels good to have the butterscotch. That sense of certainty is coming from within, and it's based on my feelings when eating butterscotch versus mint.

I want you to notice how *you* feel about small things. If, for example, someone offers you a cup of tea at the office, how do you respond? At the time of writing this chapter, we've had all sorts of changes to the way we work, so you may not be going into an office. But I know that you can remember a time when you *were* in an office, and I want you to imagine when you might say yes versus no and how easily that answer comes up for you. If someone says, "Do you feel like a cup of tea?" Are you just saying yes on autopilot? Or is there a reason you are certain you want the tea, maybe because tea would be a nice break, and you love how it tastes. Once again, I'm using small examples on purpose.

These are great questions to essentially get to know yourself. When you know all these tiny things in your life that you can be really certain with, it becomes an incredible training ground for feeling certain about the bigger things. Practice using your certainty muscle by asking yourself, "Do I feel like it? Will this make me feel good right now? Or am I just on autopilot mode?"

When you can practice with a cup of tea or flavors of chocolate, you get clear and certain about what feels great to you. Then, when it comes to the bigger things where you're craving more confidence, you'll find that your certainty muscle has been built, and that your system has become used to saying *yes* to *your* feelings.

When your system is accustomed to knowing your feelings, knowing what feels good, and knowing what feels certain, then becoming more confident in all areas become easier. Just like joy is a muscle you can build, confidence, too, comes from training deep within. That training has to come from a place of you being certain about *you*. You don't need to be certain about this or that thing. You can stand up and speak, for example, about a topic that you don't know a lot about, but you could deliver it with a lot of confidence if you're certain about *you*. You'll notice the more certain you become, your relationship with busy transforms too.

When you know yourself really well, you can start to use your feelings as a compass in your life. Confidence does not equal always feeling comfortable. You may be confident and have certainty in yourself, but still be nervous. You can still have adrenaline running through you. You may still be uncomfortable with whatever it is you're changing or doing differently. Change and growth can feel uncomfortable at times, or in fact, all of the time.

Brooke Castillo, who runs the Life Coach School in the U.S. says, "Discomfort is the currency of your dreams." And I love this quote because—you are always going to feel a bit uncomfortable if you are creating what you want in your life. You are always going to feel a touch of uncertainty if you are growing and evolving. That's natural. You can still feel confident, though, because confidence comes from *certainty in yourself.* You can be confident about the direction of travel because you know how it's going to make you feel. You can identify a feeling that is about discomfort around growth versus a feeling of discomfort that tells you, *I shouldn't do this,* or *this is not what I'm meant to be doing.*

Practice using this as your compass. When you get to know little things, like your favorite flavor of chocolate, with certainty, you can then bring that certainty to other decisions and projects you may feel less confident about. You can start to use your feelings to guide you on bigger decisions by asking yourself:

- What could make me feel a little bit more certain?

- What is it that I'm worried about?
- Is it that I'm worried what people will think?
- How can I draw on my feeling that tells me if I'm certain in myself, it doesn't matter what other people think?

I'll summarize by saying that confidence comes from a feeling of certainty in yourself. It comes from knowing what you want and creating clarity around that, which is really a process of getting to know yourself. From that self-knowledge comes your decision-making power, which is based in how you want to feel and how you do feel. When you have an awareness of your true feelings, that becomes a compass in your life, guiding you and amplifying your confidence.

Chapter 14:

Getting Cyclical About Life

Everything is going well in your life.

You've managed to make it to your weekly yoga class, things at work feel like they're running smoothly, and your schedule is on track.

Then, out of the blue, you arrive at work one day to find that everything is in chaos. Your world feels like it's falling apart. Project deadlines are missed, and suddenly, your life is stressful again.

You go through a period of three weeks of not managing to exercise at all, and you're driving yourself crazy.

When you look at the big picture, you feel like you're taking one step forward and three steps backward.

What's going on?

Why do we have these patterns where things go really well, and then they don't?

For me, this used to happen a lot: I'd feel like I had a really cool routine and rhythm to my life. I'd be meal planning and exercising. Everything would be in sync. Then I'd go on holiday. And the holiday would be wonderful and relaxing. But when I'd return, it would take me weeks or even months to get back on track. That would annoy and frustrate me. I began to wonder why would I ever even take a break if it took me so long to get back in the swing of things.

You can see how that mentality may start to creep into your life. Why would we want to stop what we're doing, particularly if things are going really well?

Another issue I've seen show up for myself and my clients is a feeling of running out of time. If you're constantly feeling like there's not enough time to get through everything, or you feel frantic at the end of the day or at the end of the year, then what I'm about to share will help you.

If you've experienced any of the above, then it's time you started **getting cyclical about your life**.

It's interesting that we get frustrated when results don't keep improving, when routines and schedules get messed up, or when suddenly the workout that we've been doing for months that has been great doesn't feel like it's giving us the same energy and muscle growth anymore. Life is not constant. Life is ever-moving, ever-changing, ever-evolving. So it's only natural that our results too will be ever-moving, ever-changing, ever-evolving. It's only natural that our routines will be ever changing and evolving.

Think about the cycles that exist in your life. I am thinking about what worked for me personally in my university days. What time I got up, what time I went to sleep, and how I approached my learning is completely different to what works for me now. Life itself is not constant; it's always changing. So too, are you.

Think of how much has changed since you were a baby. The 50 trillion cells that make up your body are constantly renewing themselves. Your biggest organ, your skin, will be completely new in a few weeks, while all of your blood cells will have passed away and been renewed in one year's time. So there's a lot of change inside us and all around us all the time.

I want to invite you to see this change as part of life. It is exactly the same in nature, which is particularly evident if you live in a very seasonal climate. I grew up in the tropics, so the change from summer to fall to winter to spring, and so on, was subtle. When I moved to a more seasonal environment, I remember running around like a kid in a playground with my friend Amparo because we were seeing autumn leaves for the very first time. We picked up bundles and threw them in the air because it was so exciting to us to see in nature this seasonal transition taking shape before our eyes.

Nature itself is ever-changing and ever-evolving, and we don't question it. It just is. It's exactly the same in our businesses or careers. I'm sure that you have some sort of process in your place of work that is ever-changing. Maybe it's a quarterly review process. Maybe it's that one project starts, then finishes, and you move on to the next. Nothing is constant.

If you're feeling particularly stressed about the results you're getting, or you're feeling frustrated that something isn't working for you anymore, I want to introduce this way of thinking into your life: *this is how it's meant to be.* Whatever you're experiencing in your life is how it's meant to be. Because life itself is not constant. You are not constant. How you approached things yesterday, with the lessons and insights and experiences of yesterday, will work differently today.

When I understood that this, too, is how personal growth works, so much pressure was released for me. I started to feel more certain about the 'goals' I had because I knew it was natural for them to shift and change too. It's what I teach all my clients in my 'Seasons of Self-Growth' system.

Also, this: you're unique. Really unique. The fact that our fingerprints are so individual to us is incredible to me. But your uniqueness extends beyond your physical body to your mental and emotional capacity. How you see the world. How you show up in the world. Your unique talents. Your gifts, your experiences, your skillset. All of these are unique to you. You are one in a trillion. If you're so unique, then surely what makes sense to you is super unique. What routines, rhythms, and schedules work for you are going to be unique to you.

I am one of these people who has always been an early bird. I love getting up early, and I love going to bed early. One of my best friends has always been a night owl. It was fun when we were studying together because we'd always have to find a compromise. Some mornings I made her get up early, and some evenings she made me stay up late.

We are so unique, and yet we try to fit ourselves into a box. If we're told that we must get up early in the mornings and do a magical morning ritual, we try it. But that may not be right for you, your temperament, or your physique. And that's okay. Find something that works for you.

I once tried an exercise bootcamp where they do all sorts of different activities like running and strength training, and there's a trainer telling you to go faster and harder. This is something that I probably would have never considered doing in my life before because it didn't naturally appeal to me. Yet, at this particular point in time, I'd been invited along and for some reason I said yes.

On the very first day, we were asked to do pushups. I'm not sure I'd ever done a pushup in my life before. If I had, I'd certainly never been *taught* to do it. I did a couple of pushups, and the trainer came past and said to me, "No, you're cheating. Stop and do some more." I thought, *What? I'm not cheating! I'm not trying to get out of this; I have no idea what you're talking about.* I wanted to quit immediately; it completely put me off. The next day I went along because I'd committed to the whole thing, although the boot camp mentality of *go harder, go faster*, turned me off. But the next day, there was a different trainer. We began doing some laps; I had to run for eight minutes straight. Now, I'm not a runner; eight minutes is a very long time for me, and it was the first time in my life I had to keep moving at that pace for that amount of time. I'd done one or two laps when I heard the new trainer yell out to me, "Come on, Danielle! You're doing really great! Keep going. You can do it." There was something in me that wanted to keep going in response, even though it wasn't my natural tendency, and even though I knew I'd probably never do a bootcamp again. The way in which she approached it flicked the switch for me in terms of my motivation. I learned that the encouragement worked for me. The thing that happened on day one, the drill sergeant mentality, did not work for me. It switched me off and shut me down. Do you know your unique motivation style? What gets you going in your life personally and professionally?

If my partner were told that he was cheating and to keep doing more pushups and *drop and give me twenty*, that would get him going. He's driven by that motivation style. There's no right or wrong here. It's simply what's unique to you.

Bootcamp or marathon training never really appealed to me. I tried my hardest through various school sports opportunities; I was always the person to give it a go. I'd even show up for cross-country running days. But what I found over time, after trying lots of different exercise routines, was when I rocked up into a yoga room, I finally felt at home.

There was something about the style, the technique, the rhythm that really felt right to my particular body. It had a lot to do with the teachers I was exposed to as well. Naturally, I then gravitated toward more of that style of movement.

For some people, the thought of being in a yoga room just doesn't work for them. For some people, the thought of being at a bootcamp just doesn't work for them, while for others, it's incredibly motivating and joyful. So once again, this is an area to find what works for you. Instead of following some "Ten Steps to Perfect Health" blog post about how you must, for example, run five miles a day to be in optimum health, tune into what feels good to you.

This is relevant to getting cyclical about your life because what's necessary to you personally could change. Even though I love yoga, and it's something that has brought me much strength, health, and wellness, it doesn't mean that I rock up on the mat every single day. In fact, I can go for months without doing any form of physical yoga whatsoever. Yet there are other periods of my life where every single day I'm doing at least a 20-minute sequence. The style of motivation that works for us can change too.

What's important to know is that we can go through these cyclical changes. When we don't acknowledge this, busyness takes a strong hold. We tell ourselves we need to 'fix' something, so we keep doing more. What we need in certain moments can change. What feels good to us in certain moments can change. **And that's okay.** So instead of beating myself up during times I'm not doing yoga, I simply notice some of the shifts that happen inside of me and recognize that I'm in a new phase. I used to think that it was me not following through on certain things, but that's not true. With the bootcamp, I followed through. Then I moved on to another activity. I've been through phases where swimming or netball was my thing. I'm giving exercise examples here because I think you'll relate. I think we've all gone through periods of trying to figure out the thing that gets us moving.

Know your personal cycles. This ties in with knowing that you're unique, figuring out your rhythm, and knowing it's okay to shift between things. Also, knowing your own personal cycles helps you to sync up your success.

So instead of fighting and stressing about the times I'm not making it into a yoga room, for example, I now know that's part of my personal cycle. Sometimes it works really well; sometimes I need a different form of it; sometimes I need a lot of child's pose; sometimes I need a lot of movement.

Knowing your own cycles can mean a lot of different things. Maybe it's knowing your own cycle in terms of your job. Maybe there's a cyclical nature to how often your projects come up. Maybe there's a cyclical nature to how you feel stressed at the start of a project. Or maybe you're someone who feels stressed at the end of a project. Are you someone who leaves things to the last minute? Or are you someone who needs a lot of preparation and planning before you go into a meeting, for example? This is what I mean by knowing your personal cycles to sync your success.

Knowing your own personal feminine cycle can be powerful too. We go through a lot of energetic changes, physical changes, and emotional changes throughout our menstrual cycle that can really help us tap into an energy of creativity or an energy of getting things done. The more you're aware of what that looks like and feels like to you personally, the more you're able to tailor your decisions to sync up your success. I've learned so much about my personal energy cycle from Kate Northrup, founder and CEO of Origin® Collective and author of *Do Less: A Revolutionary Approach To Time And Energy Management For Ambitious Women*. Adding this layer to my approach to goal-setting and self-growth cycles has been game-changing for me.

It could also be that there's a cyclical nature to how you live at home. Maybe you know that you're a morning person, and your partner's not a morning person. Knowing that difference can help you to make some simple tweaks to your schedule, and it could help you release any frustration. Or it could help you to plan out your diary in a more supportive way.

I believe that the more you know about your own personal preferences, cycles, and rhythms, the more it provides you with a sense of relief. You can know that this is **not** you stuffing up, doing a bad job, or underperforming. It's your nature; it's life. Life is going through phases. This is just another phase, and you can appreciate the phase that you're in. That gives a sense of relief. *It's supposed to be like this.*

When I know some of my peaks, some of my troughs, some of the things that work well for me, and some that don't, I have guidance pillars. When I know there's an ebb and flow to my days, weeks, and months, it gives me a sense of inner guidance. I know that I can make choices that help me sync with my personal cycle. These choices help me create a life that feels successful, joyful, easy, and prosperous. I'm guided to trusting that it's what it's meant to be, and that I'm so unique only I can make decisions for me. I don't have to mold and shapeshift myself into someone else's version of what I should be.

And with that comes certainty.

With that guidance comes the true sense of comfort and clarity that we're all craving.

Learning more about the cycles in nature, in my personal being, in life itself, has supported me to align with how I want to be living. I align with ease, flow, and joy when I remember how we are all unique, and I can trust my cycles. Any frustration melts away, and I feel in control again.

One simple question that I'll leave you with is:

What do I already know?

What do I already know about myself? About my cycle, about my rhythms, about my routines?

Brainstorm on a piece of paper and come up with everything you already know. It could be simple things, like, "I know I like early mornings and early nights. I know that yoga is much more my style than running. I know that swimming feels good for me, but running does not. I know that I'm motivated by people being gentle and encouraging." Write down anything that you know about you. I want you to notice your patterns. And once you start peeling back those layers, take a step back, and return to that brainstorming page a day or two later. You'll start to notice a rhythm, a cyclical nature to some of the things you wrote down. Which can really take the pressure off "busy". All of these juicy treasures really help shape how you can then show up and start creating a life that really lights you up, reclaiming your joy.

Chapter 15:

How to Choose Joy When You'd Rather Have a Tantrum

I just finished writing this chapter.

And it was incredible.

It was all about connecting back to a place of joy. Why joy matters. Why it's so important to you. I shared examples of the best decisions I've ever made in my life. It was much longer than this chapter will be.

It turns out there was a technical glitch with my computer, and I lost the entire chapter.

It's gone.

When I realized I had managed to accidentally erase the chapter, I felt my body crumpling and going, *oh no*.

I had a moment of choice.

Now, I'm not going to lie. I was standing at this fork in the road, and what I *really* wanted to do was crumple, stomp my feet, go run to my partner, and have a good old cry.

I also knew that I had just written a chapter about the power of having a place to come back to, a center. I wrote about why joy is not only a nice-to-have, but why it's actually a powerful tool you can choose for connecting back into your root structure, a place of grounded calmness inside. I realized that would mean I had a choice in that moment—the moment I realized I had lost the first draft of this chapter.

I asked myself this question:

What would choosing joy look like right now?

The moment I asked that question, the intensity of wanting to stomp my feet and have a good old cry softened immediately. It did not go away. I still had a tiny lump in my throat. And I did need to release that energy. However, the intensity softened very quickly—almost instantly. I walked through the house to find my partner. I chose to tell him about what happened calmly, and I did have a few soft tears at the back of my throat and a feeling of frustration. But then they went away quickly. And it's because I asked myself:

What do I want to choose? How could I choose joy in this moment?

When I asked myself those questions, immediately relief came, along with some responses.

One of the responses that came up for me was *turn the computer off and don't worry about it.* Choosing joy could mean *you don't have to write this chapter. What if you really celebrate what you've already done?* This is the other thing that came up when I asked myself those questions: *what's the lesson here? Why don't you jump back on and share that lesson?* Hence, why I'm writing this again.

I'm going to write a shorter version of what I've just written that was lost. These are the moments that matter. These moments sometimes feel like they're small, and they don't matter, and yet they can be powerful for shifting energy.

One of the things we talk about all the time in my Joy Club, which I'll tell you about later in this chapter, is that **when I talk about joy, I'm not saying to push all your other feelings aside.** What I have already written about joy in this book and what I'm sharing with you here is a process to *expand your capacity to feel.* It's a process to deepen your relationship with *all* the emotions in your life. Emotions are really cool; they give us our experience of life. So why would we want to turn them off?

Small, disappointing moments are the moments to welcome **all** the emotions. I wasn't saying, *go away, frustration and tantrum*. What I was saying is, *I have a choice right now*. Knowing that I had a choice dissipated some of the emotion immediately. It was almost like that frustration and anger was tapping at the door saying, LOOK AT ME LOOK AT ME LOOK AT ME. When I said, *hey, I have a choice*, the emotion went, *okay yeah, I can relax a little bit*.

When we're hooked on busy, we miss the opportunity to be more *responsive* and instead *react*. It's our way of numbing those uncomfortable feelings before they really hit us. Yet there's magic we miss in those feelings.

Where could you welcome more of your emotions? Where are you trying to hold back on some pain, frustration, or challenge, when actually, you could welcome the question:

How could I choose joy?

Not, "I must choose joy right now," but "*How* could I?"

What does that do to the intensity of some of the emotions for you?

It's not what you do, it's how you do it.

I still got up from my chair and told my partner about what had happened. I could have gone and told him the first way I wanted to, which was to throw a tantrum. But I didn't. I chose how I showed up. I was intentional about the tone I used and the words I said to him because I knew that would set the tone for the rest of the evening.

It's not what you do, it's how you do it is another common theme in the conversations we have in Joy Club. Often our natural reflex, particularly if we are used to wanting to progress, wanting to learn and grow, and having a desire to achieve, is to push, go, and not let go until we are there. And even when we're there, we're looking for the next thing. We say or think things like, *tell me what to do, and I'll do it.* I could give you a ten-point action plan right now for how to connect back to your place of joy. And I guarantee you that every single person who followed the plan would have an entirely different experience of it because *it's not what you do, it's how you do it.*

In Joy Club, we talk a lot about the *how* we're showing up. The *how* you are showing up comes from a place of practicing those feelings in your body.

Because I'm really conscious of my joy, because I'm really conscious of what makes me feel good, I knew in that moment when I realized the first draft of this chapter was really and truly gone, that I also had a choice. My mixture of feelings was familiar to me. I can predict what's going to roll out if I choose the frustration and tantrum. I also know what's going to roll out if I'm intentional about my word choice. I know what's going to roll out if I ask my body *what do you want right now?*

One of the things my body suggested was to not worry about this chapter—to leave it out or come back to it later. One of the other things it suggested was to share my lessons. That felt really good to me, so I showed up and did that option.

Joy doesn't just show up. I mean, sure it can, if you pay attention to it. But often, particularly if you have been on the busy train, or the productivity wheel, and you are at a junction of wanting to show up differently in your life, it starts with being **intentional about joy**.

Joy is the conversation that we're missing when it comes to stress management, career change, and even self-care. These days, we're talking about caring for ourselves and having more me time, and we're talking about the health impacts of too much stress; however, how much are we talking about joy? Are we talking about how we have to create it intentionally?

When you first learn something, like how to ride a bicycle, how to read, or how to do a new job, it feels clunky at first because you're being super conscious about it. I think about it like the quadrants or sections of the popular 'conscious-competence' learning model often used in management and leadership contexts. One quadrant we move through is being consciously incompetent. You know that you can't really do this thing. Then, as you develop, learn, and keep trying, you move into conscious competence. You know you can do it if you focus on it. Then that turns into unconscious competence, i.e., it's automatic, and you don't even have to think about it. You could almost do it blindfolded. You don't have to think about how to send a text or an email anymore, right? It just happens. Finally, there's another quadrant: unconscious incompetence, where you actually don't know what you're doing, and you don't know that you don't know what you're doing.

From a personal growth perspective, what's important is that our learning keeps going around this cycle too, through each of the four quadrants. When learning something, you have to be conscious about it. In order to grow, in order to make it automatic, in order for you to be become unconsciously competent, it has to start from a place of conscious awareness of this thing you are learning or changing. In this case, be conscious of your joy. Be intentional about how you choose joy. When you're living and leading intentionally from a place of joy, that is where transformation happens.

I'm writing this chapter at the end of 2020. As a whole, 2020 has felt like constant change. Yes, change is our natural state; we are always changing. However, in 2020 with the global pandemic, there were likely bigger disruptions or bigger adjustments to your way of life than ever before. Change can be a beautiful thing. No matter what is going on for you right now, no matter how grounded or ungrounded you feel, no matter how certain or uncertain things feel, this is a moment to take a deep breath, let it all out, and set yourself an intention of how you would like things to be.

How could you choose joy in this moment?

Community and connection are also important to our joy.

Community and connection are strategies in my life for keeping me grounded in my joy and knowing that I am safe and supported. Whether I'm having a challenging, stressful day or a joyful day worth celebrating, I create space to do that through community.

If you want to create a community to foster more joy and help you choose joy, then Joy Club may be for you. Joy Club is my membership community—a simple practice in your life of having a supportive, safe community of heart-centered women who are all going through different types of change, transition, and transformation in their lives. Joy Club members want to be intentional about choosing joy. If you want to find out more or get on the wait list so you know exactly when the doors are next opening, you can do that at www.TheDaisyPatch.co.uk/joy.

BONUS CHAPTER:

Overthinking and Getting Unstuck

You're joining me in the park where I'm on a coffee date with myself.

I've been sitting on a patch of grass in the sunshine, and there are a few things that have been going on in my mind and heart. So I'm getting my thoughts out from the park while everything is still fresh.

Last night I hosted a live Q&A for one of our Joy Club sessions. We ended up having a conversation about overthinking, how it can start to take control of our lives, and how it can happen in all sorts of different ways. We had people saying that sometimes when they're in overthinking mode, they get a sick feeling in their stomach, or when they're in overthinking mode, they find themselves procrastinating and not wanting to deal with whatever the thing is, whether it's a decision or having a tough conversation with someone. We talked about some of the things we can do to get us **out** of overthinking so that we don't feel trapped by it.

I've been thinking a lot about overthinking. In fact, perhaps I've been *overthinking about overthinking.* But it's for your benefit because I've got some great guidance to share in this bonus chapter.

I'm going to share a sneak preview of what the Joy Club conversation was like last night, and I'm going to offer a few invitations for looking at things a bit differently right now, whatever is going on for you, and whether you're reading as soon as this book comes out, or in the months or years to come. What I'm about to share will always be relevant for anyone in a transition period or uncertain time or wanting to make a change.

When we get into overthinking mode, we're getting into a stage of wanting to claw back a sense of control in our lives. Overthinking comes because we're trying to feel more certain. Our brain is telling us, *if I could just fathom this one out, if I could rationalize it, if I had all the information, then maybe, just maybe, I would feel better about it.* In some ways, overthinking is a strategy we use to not *feel* anything else going on around us. (Just like busyness). We think if we could just get on top of it, then we would feel better, and we'd have our sense of control back.

What we talked about in our Joy Club conversation about control is that there are different ways to get control. If you're reaching for control through overthinking, what tends to happen is that the control is **momentary**. You might put off stress or worry for a moment. Then you wake up the next morning, and it's still there; you're still in overthinking mode. Or we can get back control from a place where whatever we're doing to feel certain, safe, and comfortable, we could keep doing over and over again. In other words, there are resourceful ways to get a sense of safety and control in our lives, and there are unresourceful ways.

What I mean about being resourceful is that it's the *way* in which we get back in control rather than *what* exactly we do. Resourceful means that the way in which I go about handling something is sustainable. I could do it over and over again. I've tapped into a sustainable fuel source. It's not harming anyone. An unresourceful approach is short-lived; the effect is not long-lasting. I always think of procrastination when I think of unresourceful strategies because procrastination is something we do to feel better and more in control. We think, *no, I'm not going to do that thing right now, I'm going to go over here and reply to these emails instead. Because when I'm doing the emails, I feel great. I know how to do this; it's so easy for me; I'm in control.* Then you finish the emails, and that thing you have to deal with is still there. You get to feel good for a while, but inevitably you end up having to deal with that thing anyhow.

What if there was a different way for you to get back control?

What we started to tap into during the Joy Club conversation last night was thinking about what we really have control over. I wrote about this in Chapter 11, and it's worth mentioning again here.

Always, the only thing that we ultimately have control over is ourselves and anything that is born out of the self.

What's going on inside of me that I have some control over?

- What I'm telling myself
- The story that I'm coming up with
- The meaning I'm attaching to things
- The words that I choose to say out loud
- The thoughts inside my head
- The emotions that come up for me

I don't have control over what date my boss sets a deadline. I could negotiate, but I don't necessarily have control over their decision. I don't have control over another person's reaction to what I say to them and how they interpret my words. I don't even have control over my partner's mood. You can affect someone and support them, but you cannot necessarily change how they're feeling. That change comes from them. There's a fine line between influence and control, but I'm talking about the kind of control where you cannot ever actually control another person's behaviors, thoughts, or reactions to something.

My invitation here is to ask yourself, *how could I choose a more resourceful strategy for handling stress and periods of change?* Turn the spotlight onto you and ask yourself: **What part of this is in my control?**

Here are two questions I use to help myself come back to what's in my control:

What's this really about?

This is a tough question that gets straight to the heart of things.

I find that when I ask myself this question, often a theme comes up. For me, it tends to be the same stuff over and over again: I'm worried what people will think, and I'm worried about whether I'm doing something well enough. When you can get yourself to this level of detail, you can come back to a core place. This puts the spotlight back on you, and it puts you back in control. Now you know where to operate from instead of trying to fix, say, other people's deadlines or emotions. You can come back to what it's really about.

The second question is:

What's the story I'm telling myself?

What are the exact words that you're conjuring up in your head? What have you made it mean?

My story may be, *I'm worried that if I do XYZ, someone's going to think I'm a terrible businesswoman.* If I'm overthinking, I'm telling myself that story **inside** my head. I'm not getting it out or processing it in any other way.

Consider how you can process your story in another way. If you're feeling stuck in your head, anything that will get you out of your head, like moving your body, talking the worry through out loud, putting pen to paper, or any way of externalizing it will help. I'm an external processor, so whenever I chat things out with someone, I feel a new level of clarity kick in.

Emotions are kind of like a toddler tugging at mummy's skirt. *Hello. Hello. Hello. Mum. Mum, Mum, Mum.* The more you say, "Not now, not now," the louder and more intense they get until they completely melt down. I'm sure you've had the experience of trying to pause your feelings or put them on hold, and that only makes them intensify even more. According to brain scientist Dr. Jill Bolte Taylor, each emotion we feel has a chemical response in our bodies with an effect that lasts for only 90 seconds. You may not want to sit with confusion, worry, shame, anger, frustration, or whatever emotion you're trying to avoid by staying in your head and overthinking. But now that you know that each emotion only lasts for 90 seconds, could you invite yourself to sit with each of them?

When that feeling you're not wanting to feel comes in, could you say, "Okay, how can I sit with this? Can I count to 90 and sit with the discomfort?" Tell yourself, "It's safe for me to be uncomfortable. It's safe for me to feel this right now." You'll notice a shift; maybe it won't be a sudden release or relief, but it will change. And in that change, you'll be able to suddenly see things with more clarity. I wrote more about emotions in Chapter 8.

If you find yourself questioning, worrying, or trying to plan things in the future that are uncertain, come back to this:

The only thing you have control over in your life is you. Other words for control are certainty, safety, and comfort. You can gain these things in a resourceful, sustainable way. When you do, you will get your time and energy back because you won't be leaking it by running less resourceful strategies.

You'll be free from busy.

Acknowledgements

This book came about by chance, and deep trust. I didn't set out to write a book in 2020, and yet, here it is!

It couldn't have been birthed into the world, right at a time when it most needed to be heard, without the generous support and encouragement of my Editor, friend, and mastermind sister, Genevieve Parker Hill.

While there are numerous other souls who have contributed to me being in this place right now, able to share this message, it was Genevieve's words of genuine enthusiasm and belief in my work that meant I even considered the idea in the first place.

Words do little to express how much her energy and prowess have guided me and enabled this creation.

From the depths of my heart, thank you.

About the Author

Life Coach, wellness enthusiast, and practical positive thinker, Danielle Brooker, is the host of *The Let it Shine* podcast and founder of *The Daisy Patch*. There, she creates conversations about creating more joy in our lives, navigating tough decisions, and allowing ourselves to shine.

Through her private coaching programs, digital courses, and monthly Joy Club membership, she's redefining the conversation on stress and "busyness"—supporting highly ambitious, stressed-out women to reclaim their lives from busy and step into their joy.

She lives in her dream city, London, with her partner, Nathan. To learn more about Danielle and her work visit www.thedaisypatch.co.uk.

Printed in Great Britain
by Amazon